# Churchill

## Professor J. Rufus Fears

THE TEACHING COMPANY ®

**PUBLISHED BY:**

**THE TEACHING COMPANY**
**4840 Westfields Boulevard, Suite 500**
**Chantilly, Virginia 20151-2299**
**1-800-TEACH-12**
**Fax—703-378-3819**
**www.teach12.com**

Copyright © The Teaching Company, 2001

Printed in the United States of America

This book is in copyright. All rights reserved.

Without limiting the rights under copyright reserved above,
no part of this publication may be reproduced, stored in
or introduced into a retrieval system, or transmitted,
in any form, or by any means
(electronic, mechanical, photocopying, recording, or otherwise),
without the prior written permission of
The Teaching Company.

ISBN 1-56585-862-X

# J. Rufus Fears, Ph.D.

## Professor of Classics, University of Oklahoma

J. Rufus Fears is Professor of Classics at the University of Oklahoma, where he holds the G. T. and Libby Blankenship Chair in the History of Liberty. He rose from Assistant Professor to Professor of History at Indiana University. From 1986 to 1990, he was Professor of Classics and Chairman of the Department of Classical Studies at Boston University.

Professor Fears holds the Ph.D. from Harvard University. He has been a Danforth Fellow, a Woodrow Wilson Fellow, and a Harvard Prize Fellow. He has been a Fellow of the American Academy in Rome, a Guggenheim Fellow, and twice a Fellow of the Alexander von Humboldt Foundation. His research has been supported by grants from the American Philosophical Society, the American Council of Learned Societies, the National Endowment for the Humanities, the Kerr Foundation, and the Zarrow Foundation. He was chosen as Indiana University's first Distinguished Faculty Research Lecturer. He is listed in *Who's Who in America* and *Who's Who in the World*.

Professor Fears is the author of more than 70 articles and reviews on Greek and Roman history, the history of liberty, and the lessons of history for our own day. His books and monographs include *Princeps A Diis Electus: The Divine Election of the Emperor as a Political Concept at Rome*, *The Cult of Jupiter and Roman Imperial Ideology*, *The Theology of Victory at Rome*, and *The Cult of Virtues and Roman Imperial Ideology*. He has published a three-volume edition of *Selected Writings of Lord Acton*, the great British historian of liberty. He has lectured widely in the United States and Europe, and his scholarly work has been translated into German and Italian.

Professor Fears is very active in speaking to broader audiences, and his comments on the lessons of history for our own day have appeared on television and been carried in newspapers and journals throughout the United States and abroad. Of the many study trips he leads to historical sites in the United States and Europe, the most popular is "Winston Churchill and World War II."

On 15 occasions, Dr. Fears has received awards for outstanding teaching. In 1996, 1999, and again in 2000, he was chosen the University of Oklahoma Professor of the Year.

*Churchill* is the fourth course Professor Fears has produced with The Teaching Company. *Famous Greeks* and *Famous Romans* are introductions to classical Greek and Roman history through the lives of the great men and women who made that history. *A History of Freedom* is a 36-lecture survey of the events, ideas, and institutions of liberty from classical antiquity to our own day.

©2001 The Teaching Company.

# Table of Contents
# Churchill

©2001 The Teaching Company.

# Churchill

**Scope:**

Winston Churchill was the greatest leader of the 20$^{th}$ century. He is proof that a single individual can change the course of history. His courage, character, and genius rallied the British people to "their finest hour." His was a multifaceted genius. He was a successful politician and a statesman of vision and principle. He was a military innovator, who outpaced his contemporaries in his grasp of the impact of technology on warfare. He was one of the most successful authors of his day, who won the Nobel Prize for Literature. He was a painter, whose artistic work brought him a considerable income during his life and still hangs today in major museums. With all this, he was a father who won the devotion of his children. Our course is a narrative of the life and achievements of Winston Churchill and an analysis of the qualities that made him a great leader and a great man.

Our course begins at the supreme moment in Churchill's life, his address to Parliament on June 4, 1940, declaring to the world that Britain "shall never surrender." As Churchill later wrote, his whole past life "had been but a preparation for this hour and this trial." The man who so rallied a nation in the cause of democracy was born into wealth and privilege, the descendant of John Churchill, Duke of Marlborough. Lecture One examines the career of this extraordinary soldier and statesman and his importance for understanding Winston Churchill.

Lectures Two and Three look at the early life of Winston Churchill and show how "a troublesome boy" emerged by age 26 as a war hero, best-selling author, millionaire, and member of Parliament. Lectures Four treats Churchill's early political career. We explore his democratic ideals and his concern for the ordinary person. We watch his meteoric rise to become First Lord of the Admiralty by age 37 and witness his tragic fall as a result of the failed Dardanelles (Gallipoli) campaign in 1915. Lecture Five takes the Dardanelles campaign as a springboard to discuss Churchill's character as a political leader and those qualities that won him so many enemies and critics, as well as admirers. The decade following World War I saw Churchill emerge again as a leading figure in British politics; Lecture Six assesses his seminal role in issues that continue to be at the center of wold politics today: Northern Ireland and the Middle East.

It is in the wholeness of his achievements and personality that we find so much to admire in Churchill. Lecture Seven describes his life as a devoted father, best-selling author, and successful painter. Lectures Eight through Ten focus on the critical moment in the life of Churchill and the history of the 20th century: his leadership of Britain in the mighty struggle against Hitler. We judge his achievements as a statesman and as a wartime leader of a democracy. It is truly a study of leadership in a time of crisis. Foresight is one of the chief qualities of a statesman. Lecture Eleven examines how, in the years following World War II, both out of office and as Prime Minister for a second time, Churchill strove to achieve his vision of peace and freedom, resting on a united Europe, close relations with America, and a viable coexistence with the Soviet Union.

Churchill was a genius and a man of principle. Accordingly, he never lacked for critics. In life, he was attacked by mediocre critics in politics and the press. In death, historians from a wide range of political opinions have assailed him. Our concluding lecture listens to the critics of Churchill and answers them with the simple facts of his achievements and the enduring principles of his political philosophy.

This course rests on the most recent historical scholarship. It is thoroughly documented by Churchill's own writings and speeches. After all this study, we conclude as we began, with the view that Winston Churchill was the greatest figure of the 20th century.

©2001 The Teaching Company.

# Lecture One
# Heritage and Destiny

**Scope:**

On June 4, 1940, Winston Churchill addressed the British Parliament. Barely three weeks had passed since he became Prime Minister. The time was what some call "the darkest days in English history." The Nazis had conquered the Low Countries, and France was falling. Hitler was convinced that Britain, too, would make a negotiated peace. To Parliament and the world, Churchill proclaimed, "We shall never surrender." With this speech, Churchill rallied his nation and began the march toward ultimate victory in the most titanic war in history. Churchill is arguably the greatest leader of the 20th century and perhaps the greatest Englishman in history. Our course examines the life and achievements of this multifaceted genius, who won the Nobel Prize for Literature and whose paintings have been deemed worthy to hang in major museums of the world.

This man who would change the course of history was born to wealth and privilege on November 30, 1874, in Blenheim Palace. Our course begins, as Churchill would have begun, with the legacy of heroism and public service he received from his famous ancestor, John, Duke of Marlborough, and from his own father, Lord Randolph Churchill.

# Outline

I.  When Churchill died in January 1965, Clement Attlee said that he was the greatest Englishman of our time and, perhaps, the greatest citizen of the world of our time.

    **A.** Attlee was a lifelong socialist, with political views very different from those of Churchill. However, Attlee's tribute was sincere and was taken up throughout England, the United States, and much of Europe.

    **B.** The only correction that was offered by many to Attlee's assessment was to call Churchill the greatest citizen of all time.

    **C.** This course argues that Churchill was one of those great individuals who changed the course of history.

**II.** On June 4, 1940, Winston Churchill addressed the British Parliament.

    **A.** On May 10, 1940, Churchill had become Prime Minister.
- **1.** It was a time of supreme crisis.
- **2.** The German army seemed invincible.
- **3.** In September1939, the Germans had conquered Poland.
- **4.** In April and May 1940, the Germans had occupied Norway and Denmark and conquered the Low Countries.
- **5.** The French army, thought to be the strongest in the world, was collapsing. Its collapse was the result of the failure and lack of will of the French political and military leaders.
- **6.** From May 26 to June 3, 1940, 336,000 British and French troops had been rescued at Dunkirk. However, as Churchill said, wars are not won by evacuations.

    **B.** Many at the highest level of the British government, including King George VI, thought that Britain could not win the war.
- **1.** The Foreign Secretary, Lord Halifax, thought that Britain should negotiate a peace with Nazi Germany, which would have left the British in control of their empire and Germany in control of Europe.
- **2.** The king and many others did not want Churchill as Prime Minister.
- **3.** "Shrewd" politicians, such as Halifax, wanted Churchill to be Prime Minster, to make a peace with Germany, and then, tarnished by the peace, be forced to step down.

    **C.** To the British people, to Germany and the Axis powers, to the United States, still neutral, Churchill addressed his famous words: "We shall never surrender."

**III.** With that speech, Churchill rallied a nation to "their finest hour."

    **A.** Churchill was the greatest statesman of the 20th century. He joins Pericles of Athens and Abraham Lincoln as one of the greatest statesman in the history of democracy.

    **B.** We distinguish a statesman from a politician by four criteria:
- **1.** A bedrock of principles.
- **2.** A moral compass.
- **3.** A vision.

©2001 The Teaching Company.

**4.** The ability to build a consensus to achieve that vision.

**C.** Churchill's bedrock of principles was his devotion to liberty.

**D.** Churchill's moral compass lay in his conviction of absolute right and wrong. He was ambitious, but he would not do certain things to achieve his goals if he believed such actions to be wrong.

**E.** Churchill's vision was of the entire world moving toward true freedom, liberty under the law; Churchill had an extraordinary concern for the ordinary person.

**F.** His mastery of the English language, his skill as a speaker and a writer, were fundamental to his ability to build a consensus to achieve this vision.

    **1.** Before Churchill's speech of June 4, 1940, a public opinion poll might have shown that a majority of British were opposed to another speech.

    **2.** With one speech, he changed public opinion.

**IV.** The statesman who so rallied a nation was born into wealth and privilege at Blenheim Palace, near Oxford, England, on November 30, 1874.

**A.** Churchill's life was profoundly shaped by the legacy of military and political courage he received from his famous ancestor, John, Duke of Marlborough, and Churchill's own father, Lord Randolph Churchill.

**B.** Churchill wrote superb biographies of both these figures.

**V.** John, First Duke of Marlborough (1650–1722) was one of the most gifted generals and military minds of his era and played a major role in making England a world power.

**A.** He was born the son of Sir Winston Churchill, a man of some wealth and prominence.

    **1.** John's background and ability won him advancement in royal circles.

    **2.** By the age of 25, he had distinguished himself as a soldier in England's war against Holland.

    **3.** In the winter of 1677–1678, he married Sarah Jennings, who played an important role in his political advancement.

**B.** In the service of King James II (1685–1688), John Churchill advanced in position and fortune. However, concerned by

King James's bent toward Catholicism, John betrayed the king and went over to the side of William and Mary in 1688.

C. The "Glorious Revolution" of William and Mary (1688–1702) and the reign of their successor, Queen Anne * (1702–1714), saw John Churchill reach the pinnacle of his career.
   1. In 1689, he was made Earl of Marlborough.
   2. In 1702, he was named by Queen Anne as Captain General of English troops, both at home and abroad.

D. The War of the Spanish Succession (1701–1714) was between the allied forces of Britain, Holland, and Austria against King Louis XIV of France. Marlborough was made commander-in-chief of the united troops of Holland and Britain.
   1. On August 13, 1704, Marlborough led the allied armies to victory near the German village of Blenheim.
   2. Marlborough was both a brilliant general and a superb diplomat.
   3. He served in the front ranks and looked after his men, who were devoted to him.
   4. He led his armies to further victories over the French at the Battles of Ramillies (1706), Oudenarde (1708), and Malplaquet (1709).

E. For his service, John Churchill was elevated from his status as the Earl of Marlborough to Duke of Marlborough. The royal manor at Woodstock near Oxford was given to him, and Queen Anne and Parliament built Blenheim Palace for him.

F. Court intrigues led to Marlborough's fall from power in 1711.
   1. Marlborough retained his fortune and palace, and his descendants still today hold the title and Blenheim Palace.
   2. English historians and writers, including Jonathan Swift, Henry Hallam, and Thomas Babington Macaulay attacked his reputation.

G. Winston Churchill set out to restore his ancestor's reputation in his four-volume biography, *Marlborough, His Life and Times* (1933–1938).

©2001 The Teaching Company.

**Essential Reading:**

Jones, *Marlborough*.

**Supplementary Reading:**

Churchill, *Marlborough*.

**Questions to Consider:**

1. Marlborough deserted the cause of King James to serve William and Mary. Winston Churchill twice changed parties during his political life. Do these actions make them political opportunists?

2. Marlborough is not much studied today. Do you agree that his achievements as a general and a statesman deserve far greater attention?

---

*Erratum*: Professor Fears states that Queen Anne was the daughter of William and Mary, when, in fact, she was the sister of Mary, and daughter of James II

---

# Lecture One—Transcript
## Heritage and Destiny

I want to welcome you to our course on Winston Churchill. When Churchill died in January of 1965, Clement Attlee said that he was greatest Englishman of our time, perhaps the greatest citizen of the world of our time. Now, Clement Attlee was a life long socialist. He had worked closely with Churchill during the war, but their political principles were diametrically opposed, and yet his tribute to Churchill was taken up throughout England, throughout the United States, and over much of Europe. The only correction that was offered by many was that Churchill was the greatest Englishman of all time.

As we go into the 21$^{st}$ century that judgment still stands. He was ranked the greatest Englishman of the 20$^{th}$ century; I think we can call him the greatest statesman of the 20$^{th}$ century. I have used the word "great" several times, and our course on Churchill complements our earlier courses in the *History of Freedom*, in *Famous Greeks* and in *Famous Romans*, for it is rooted in the idea that history is made by outstanding individuals, not by anonymous social and economic forces, but by titanic individuals who change the course of history. And it is the argument of this course that Churchill is one such individual.

We will begin, as Churchill did, with his family tradition of patriotism and service to England in the figure of his ancestor, John, the First Duke of Marlborough. We will look at Churchill's youth, his schooling, his relationships with his parents, and see how this "troublesome boy," as his mother called him, would achieve by, the age of twenty-six election to Parliament, a war hero, and a self-made millionaire as a best selling author. We will follow him in two lectures through his early parliamentary career, rising rapidly to become First Lord of the Admiralty, and then falling dramatically in the course of the campaign at the Dardanelles during World War I. We will see him come back into government office, but find him, by 1930, in the wilderness, a member of Parliament but with little influence. We will see him as a family man, we will see him as a painter, an author, and then we will watch as he, almost alone in England, speaks out in the late '30s against the pressing danger of Hitler and the Nazis. And then in two lectures we will see him in that moment for which destiny had prepared him: leading the British

©2001 The Teaching Company.

people to victory in the greatest of all wars. We will see him voted out of office at the very moment of his triumph, come back as Prime Minister, and live on to be a leading elder statesman, speaking out for a united England, a united Europe, and ever closer relationship between the United States and Britain, and for détente with the Soviet Union. And in our final two lectures we will assess his political thought and his place in history.

But, unlike recent American presidents, Churchill was not obsessed with his place in history. He was content to say, "I have done my best" and ultimately our assessment of him will be based on that moment when Britain stood alone against the victorious forces of Nazi Germany and he rallied his nation. I would ask you to step back to that moment, to June 4, 1940, to the House of Parliament and Winston Churchill is about to address it. Three weeks had passed since he became Prime Minister; three weeks in which England is passing through what many are calling its "darkest days." But Churchill doesn't like to call them "dark days" he calls them "stern days," but they are stern in deed. In these three weeks, the German armies have poured through the Low Countries into France, and at this point, June 4, the French army is collapsing. The French army that had fought so brave all through the First World War is now in retreat. It is surrendering in such masses that the Germans cannot even collect all the prisoners. The Belgium army as well, which fought bravely in the First World War has surrendered.

Now this is not because the French or Belgium soldiers are unwilling to fight, it is not because the French or Belgium civilian is unwilling to go through another war, it is because of a collapse of leadership at the top. The French leaders will not fight, they do not have the will to fight, and Churchill has grasped this on trips to France in which he has tried to arouse in them again a fighting spirit. And the Belgium army has been surrendered by its king, when it still wanted to fight, and that surrender by King Leopold has left some 400,000 British and French troops cut off at a little spit of land called Dunkirk.

When Churchill called this meeting at Parliament he thought he would have to deliver hard and heavy tidings of a surrender of the British army. But starting on May 27, a motley little fleet—garbage scowls, royal naval vessels, there was even a yacht piloted by an American—had made their way back and forth across the English Channel under heavy enemy fire, and they rescued some 336,000

British and French troops. It is a cause for jubilation, and yet Churchill knows wars are not won by evacuation. And those who saw these British and French troops march through the streets of Dover, read defeat in their eyes, and indeed at the highest levels of the British government there is defeatism. The Foreign Secretary, Lord Halifax, and the king himself believed that England could not win this war, that what British must do is make an negotiated peace with the Germans, a peace that will leave the British in control of their empire and the Germans in control of the Continent. It is indeed because of this defeatism that Churchill has been chosen Prime Minister. You see, a clever politician—and Lord Halifax, the Foreign Secretary, is an extremely clever politician, he would be at home today—he believed that Churchill would have to make this negotiated peace, be tarnished by it, and then have to step down.

And so, it is to a Parliament expecting to hear feelers for peace; it is to the United States not yet in the war, of course, (but told by it's ambassador, Ambassador Kennedy that England cannot last); and it is to Hitler who is convinced that the British will make a negotiated peace ("England is finished" he has told Herman Gering, "they will make a peace with me"); it is to all of these, as well as to the British people, that Churchill speaks on this June 4, 1940 and says:

> Although large tracks of Europe and many old and famous States have fallen or may fall into the grip of the Gestapo and all the odious apparatus of Nazi rule, we shall not flag or fail. We shall go on to the end, we shall fight in France, we shall fight on the seas and on the oceans, we shall fight with growing strength and confidence in the air, we shall defend our island whatever the cost may be, we shall fight on the beaches, we shall fight on the landing grounds, we shall fight in the fields and in the streets, we shall fight in the hills; we shall never surrender …

Now, a British lieutenant that had been evacuated from Dunkirk spoke of hearing those words, he said:

> We have been shattered by the panzers in France, many of my men did not even have boots any more and all of our equipment was left. We were cold and hungry, and they just dumped us on the road there in Dover. And we woke up that night screaming that the panzers were upon us again, and

then I heard Churchill speak. And I said the hell with the panzers we are going to win.

And with that speech Winston Churchill rallied the nation.

Now, had he taken a public opinion poll on June 4, 1940, 80% of the British would have said it is not worth it again, it is not worth one million dead. The First World War solved absolutely nothing and our politicians have just gotten us into the same mess. But newspapers that had been critical of him for years now rallied, they published a picture of a bulldog looking like Churchill with a little Tommy helmet on it saying, "go to it," and so the British did go to it.

Now, the man who so rallied the nation at this critical moment was a statesman. And the central part of our course is to examine: What do we mean by "statesman" and how is it embodied in Winston Churchill? For Churchill ranks with Pericles of Athens and with Abraham Lincoln of our own country as one of the three outstanding democratic statesmen in history. A statesman has a bedrock of principles, that is how we begin to distinguish a statesman from a politician—a bedrock of principles unswerving—and Churchill's were rooted in freedom. Someone who knew him well, his private secretary, said the spring of all of Mr. Churchill's actions are the ideas of freedom: an ideal of individual freedom not regimented by parties or political ideologies; a tradition of freedom under law going all the way to the Magna Carta; a deep belief in the principles embodied in our Declaration of Independence (for he regarded us and British as the two great bastions of liberty).

Secondly, a statesman has a moral compass. Now, we have antennae today; we put our antennae out and want to see what other people want us to say. But for Churchill, there was absolute right and absolute wrong. Adolph Hitler represented absolute wrong. Churchill was an ambitious man throughout his life, but there were things he would not do if they were wrong; he had a moral compass that guided him and enabled him to set priorities.

And then there must be a vision, and Churchill's was the finest of all visions: of ordinary men and women marching into the bright uplands of freedom. Clement Attlee also said Churchill had an extraordinary concern for the ordinary person, and to him that was the ultimate touchstone of freedom: Is the ordinary person secure from fear and want? Can the ordinary person play a role in government? Does the ordinary person have the same right to justice as the wealthy?

But you also must make a consensus; we must be able to build a consensus to achieve that vision. For Churchill, it was the written and spoken word; we will examine him as a master of the English prose, one of the most powerful speakers in the English language. A statesman who would win the Noble Prize for Literature and in whose very fiber the lessons of the history that he studied were engrained.

Now, this statesman who so rallied the nation was born into wealth and privilege. Born at Blenheim Palace on November 30, 1874, and that palace and the memory of its founder, John, the Duke of Marlborough, would consume Churchill. He would write a masterful biography of Marlborough from 1933 until 1938, and the career of this English soldier and statesman would be, again, part of that fiber of the lessons of history. So we start with John the Duke of Marlborough, as Churchill would have wanted us to start.

John Churchill was born in 1650, the son of Sir Winston Churchill. Sir Winston Churchill was a man of some standing, prominence, but he had all been but ruined politically, as well as financially, by the English Civil War. He was a Catholic, and he had sided with the royal party. He had fought against Parliament and for a while had to live in hiding. But, with the restoration of the royal house in 1660, Sir Winston got back part of his estate and developed very close ties with the restored king, King Charles, and was able to find, in the service of King Charles, places for two of his children, his daughter, Arabella, and his son, John. John became a page with the heir to the throne, Prince James, and Arabella became Prince James's mistress and would bear him children.

John proved himself early on, not just through his sister's connections, but by his own ability as a worthy soldier. He was commissioned into what would become the Grenadier Guards and was sent out to some of the toughest posts in Tangiers. He served as a soldier and then took service, as was quite common, in the armies of the king of France. He served under one of the most famous generals of the age. He also won the attention of King Louis himself and became very close to James after James became king. But, unlike his father, John was a protestant, he was deeply attached to the protestant religion and like other English aristocrats, even those

©2001 The Teaching Company.

close to King James, he was deeply disturbed and concerned about the king's obvious desire to re-establish Catholicism, and so he entered into negotiations with the ruler of Holland, William, Prince of Orange and also the husband of the king's daughter, Mary. He was one of the first aristocrats to offer his services and one placed to an important post because of his role in the army. And so when King James was driven out of the country and William and Mary became rulers, John was there on the spot. He also was able to play an important role through the close relationship between his wife, Sarah, and the daughter of William, Princess Anne, and that relationship would grow ever closer and closer and again play an important role in Marlborough's rise.

But he also won the attention and favor of William simply by his ability as a soldier, as a general, but even more by the broad view he took of European politics—for he alone shared, in its entirety, William's view of the danger of Louis of France. William, in many ways, had simply become King of England because it was one more way of fighting against Louis. He saw in Louis the tyranny that would spread all over Europe unless a small state like Holland resisted. He had spent much of his life fighting Louis. And now, with the resources of British behind him, William continued this war, and John Churchill served closely with him. Back in 1689, he had been raised to the rank of Earl of Marlborough, and when William died in 1702, it was the wish of the dying king that Marlborough assume command of all of the British forces. So he became, under Queen Anne, the commander-in-chief of British forces.

His policy and strategy for defeating Louis became the guiding policy of the British for the next decade. His desire was to crush the power of France and to do it by a series of campaigns on the Continent. Campaigns were the ultimate goal of establishing the British as a Continental power. Now, it was not a policy that went unchallenged. There was a strong faction in Parliament, the Tories, the Conservatives who wanted a far more isolated policy for the British: a policy that focused upon Spain, a policy that focused upon the colonies of Spain and the commerce of Britain.

But for a decade Churchill was able to fight against Louis. He was never a party man; he was never totally part of the Whigs, never totally part of the Tories. He guided, above all, by his moral authority and his success in the field. He guided a grand coalition, a grand alliance in the War of the Spanish Succession, the series of wars that by which Louis attempted to expand his power all over Europe; the grand alliance consisted of British, Holland, small states like Prussia and Baden in German, and the Holy Roman Empire, the Austrian empire of the Habsburgs. Not a ruler himself, not with a strong base in Parliament, Marlborough had to hold together this alliance. It was not an easy alliance; the Dutch merchants in Amsterdam had a very bad habit of lending money to King Louis at critical moments, enabling him to reinforce his armies. The German princes had to be encouraged year after year to give their supply of troops, and Austria was always very wary of the aims of Britain. The Austrian armies were led by one of the finest soldiers of his day, Prince Eugene of Savoy.

So it was with this difficult task that Marlborough fought to intervene against the "Continental tyrant," as his descendent Winston Churchill would call it. The great victory came in 1704. Two years, 1702 and 1703, had brought success neither to Louis and the French armies nor to the armies of the alliance. Most of the fighting was done in what we would call Belgium today, a prime goal of the expansion of Louis, until, in 1704, Marlborough took a bold plan of marching with his army out of Koblenz, where he faked an attack up the Mosel River into French territory and instead marched to the Danube.

Now this is the day of the professional army, of soldiers brought in and drilled and trained under the most brutal conditions; in which a British officer's wig cost more than an ordinary soldier might make in a lifetime; when aristocrats led the army and the ordinary soldier was considered to be the biggest oaf and the biggest drunkard and the laziest man in his village; when soldiers marched in ordered lines and magnificent uniforms to within fifty yards of each other and then fired away with their muskets and followed with a bayonet charge. It was a time when generals didn't give that much attention to the care of their ordinary soldier and the French forces tended to live off the land by foraging. But Marlborough fed his men, he saw to it that they had boots and warm clothes, and they served him with a devotion. A devotion to a general who always fought in the front ranks rights along side them. They made a march in one month from Koblenz to the Danube, and then they captured a major French fortification storming up a hill three times in the face of enemy fire for their commander. Now French generals, though famous (and the French army had a reputation for invincibility), did not take the same care and they didn't have the same attention to detail that Marlborough did. He went out constantly on reconnaissance missions, he always knew exactly where the enemy was.

So it was, on August 12, that as the evening came on, he was within two miles of the French forces. They were so careless, the French were, they simply lay down and slept that night where they were, along side the road, and could not imagine that Marlborough would bring on battle so quickly. But the next morning, August 13, 1704, near a little Bavarian village called Blenheim, he had troops prepared. Now, Marlborough was a careful student of the tactics of antiquity. He focused upon the tactics of Alexander the Great, and he absorbed one of the central lessons: to hold down both flanks of the enemy, to make them commit their resources to those flanks, thinking that is where your main charge was coming, and then to mass superior force at the critical moment in the enemies line in the center, and that is what Marlborough did.

He launched the allied troops first against the little village of Blenheim on his right flank, and then attacked the left of the French forces. So savage was the battle around the village of Blenheim that the French committed more and more resources. They were quite sure that their center, the French center was protected because a little river, the River Nebel, ran in front of it. They thought the river was unfordable; Marlborough knew different, he had indeed crossed it the night before. He sent his infantry into the center of the French line, and then attacked with the full force of his calvary, attacking in a different formation, a wedge shaped formation in which it was a thundering calvary charge. The French were accustomed to ride up with their calvary, fire their pistols and turn away. Churchill's men rode directly into the line, their sabers flashing and broke the French line. Hundreds of Frenchmen fled and dove into the Danube where they perished and 11,000 surrendered.

It was a victory that destroyed forever the myth of French invincibility and established Marlborough in the minds of his contemporaries as the greatest soldier of the age. Jubilation throughout the allies, and in Britain, Parliament passed a solemn motion by which he would become not only the Duke of Marlborough but also a palace would be built for him. The royal manor at Woodstock was given to him. And until this day, Blenheim

Palace, named in honor of the great victory, is the only residence in Britain that is called a palace that is not a royal residence. And there, designed by one of the most famous architects of the age, was built, year after year, until it stood with 2,700 acres of magnificent gardens and woods and 320 rooms, celebrating the victory of Marlborough, comparing him to Scipio Africanus—the defender of Britain, as Scipio had been the defender of Rome. Great tapestries showing his magnificent victories, not just at Blenheim, but then in succeeding years at Ramillies, Oudenarde, and Malplaquet.

But the grandeur of these victories did not bring resulting decisive success. Louis continued, sponsored in part by the Dutch merchants who were theoretically his enemy, and no lasting peace was achieved. Marlborough would spend his winters traveling to the courts of Europe, driving through the snows and rain and cold to Prussia to make sure the Prussian king sent his troops into the field, and then coming back to Britain to hold on to his Parliamentary majority. But it was not easy, his wife quarreled bitterly with Queen Anne, envy and jealousy of the achievements of Marlborough led to conspiracies against him. His supporters in Parliament were pulled down. And when he asked Queen Anne to make him captain-general of the British armies for life, she refused, and in this loss of royal favor his enemies moved. He was stripped of his offices.

Jonathan Swift, the author of *Gulliver's Travels*, was a major journalist force against Marlborough, attacking him in the most savage fashion as a man who had grown wealthy through the war and wanted only to continue the war to increase his wealth. So Marlborough would be pulled down from power, he would keep Blenheim Palace, but live the rest of his life embittered. English historians attacked him. In 1827, Henry Hallam said "nothing but ambition and rapacity in his motives, nothing but treachery and intrigue in his means." The great Macaulay the next year would write: "in no other age could the path to power and glory but open to the manifold infamies of John Churchill."

Winston Churchill set out to revise this opinion in his biography written between 1933 and 1938. He sat again upon a pedestal of greatness his ancestor, but more than that, he learned fundamental lessons. A belief that an alliance, even of a smaller state, could defeat a Continental tyrant, the need for a party base and a position of moral authority if you were going to undertake a grand crusade, but most importantly, that for Britain, the ultimate goal of foreign policy and the preservation of British liberties lay in resisting any power that sought to dominate Europe. And so from early in his parliamentary career, he would recognize the danger of Germany. Then when the war with Germany was almost won in World War II, he would point out a new Continental tyrant arising in the form of Russia. But all that lies in the future, let us go back to November 30, 1874, and the birth of Winston Churchill and Blenheim.

# Lecture Two
# Young Churchill

**Scope:**

Lord Randolph, the second son of the seventh Duke of Marlborough, was a shrewd politician and a brilliant speaker. His marriage to the American heiress Jennie Jerome produced Winston Leonard Spencer-Churchill, whose early years held little promise of future greatness. The attention of his parents was minimal and largely counterproductive. His record at school was unexceptional. It was only in his late teens, at the military college of Sandhurst, that Churchill began to come into his own.

## Outline

**I.** Throughout his career, Churchill would be hounded by false accusations and called a political adventurer, even as his ancestor John Churchill, the Duke of Marlborough, had been.

   **A.** Marlborough's only son had died as a child.

   **B.** His titles passed down through his daughter Anne, who married Charles Spencer, Earl of Sunderland.

   **C.** In this manner, Princess Diana was related to Winston Churchill.

   **D.** The descendants of the Duke of Marlborough were not especially distinguished in politics until the seventh Duke of Marlborough, John Winston Spencer-Churchill (1822–1883).

   **1.** He was a significant figure in the Conservative Party and Lord-Lieutenant of Ireland.

   **2.** His second son was Lord Randolph Churchill, the father of Winston Churchill.

**II.** Randolph Churchill was elected to Parliament in 1874.

   **A.** He was soon recognized as a brilliant speaker, shrewd parliamentarian, and a man of enormous ambition.

   **B.** He met his future wife, Jeanette (Jennie) Jerome, Winston Churchill's mother, at a party given in honor of the Prince and Princess of Wales and the future Czar of Russia, Alexis III.

C. Jennie was the daughter of Clarissa and Leonard Jerome, an extremely wealthy New York financier.

D. The Jerome family spent much time living in England and Europe.

E. Within a week after they met, Jennie and Randolph were engaged.

F. They were wed on April 15, 1874.

G. Winston Leonard Spencer-Churchill was born November 30, 1874.

H. Churchill's relations with his parents were quite unlike anything an American child of today might experience but were not unusual for the child of aristocrats in Victorian England.

    1. The political life of his father and the social life of both parents left them little time and less interest for their child.

    2. Winston spent most of his time with his nanny, Mrs. Elizabeth Anne Everest, whom he affectionately called "woom."

I. Winston's early years were spent in Ireland, where his father had been posted.

J. In 1885, Lord Randolph became Chancellor of the Exchequer and proceeded to take positions that opposed that of the Prime Minister.

K. In 1886, Lord Randolph resigned, after his budget was rejected by the Prime Minister.

L. His power began to decline, along with his physical health.

III. At age seven, Winston was sent to boarding school.

A. Winston's school record was poor, including his years at the famous "public" (we would say private) school of Harrow.

B. Winston was also lonely.

    1. His mother rarely visited him at boarding school; she even forgot his Christmas presents.

    2. His father was never sure how old he was and never visited him, even though Winston begged him to.

    3. There was no intimacy between Lord Randolph and Winston.

**C.** Despite this, Winston worshipped his father as a hero and was devoted to his mother.

**D.** Lord Randolph was so disappointed in Winston's record that he was not allowed to go to Eton, the most prestigious school and his father's alma mater. Lord Randolph had gone to Oxford University. He thought Winston unfit for either Oxford or Cambridge. Randolph thus denied his son the credentials most suited to an English aristocrat.

**E.** At Harrow, although he did poorly and was not interested in most subjects, Winston did better in history and took an interest in English.

**F.** Believing his son incapable of achieving entrance to university, Lord Randolph suggested a military career to Winston, a suggestion Winston eagerly accepted.

**G.** But Winston did not gain entrance to the Royal Military College at Sandhurst without a struggle.

**IV.** Churchill began to come into his own as a cadet at the Royal Military College at Sandhurst (1893–1894).

**A.** While there, he studied subjects that had immediate value for him and, in a class of 130, he graduated twentieth.

**B.** Even Winston's progress at Sandhurst did not endear him to his father, whose health was declining rapidly.

**C.** Lord Randolph died in 1894, the same year that Churchill graduated from Sandhurst.

**D.** Churchill later wrote that the solitary tree, if it grows at all, grows to be strong and sturdy, and frequently, a boy deprived of his father's love feels determined to win that love back, even after his father has gone. Churchill spent part of his life trying to live up to the expectations of a father who denied him that love.

**Essential Reading:**

Manchester, *Churchill I*, pp. 43–210.

**Supplementary Reading:**

Churchill, *My Early Life*, pp. 1–60; *Lord Randolph Churchill*.
Foster, *Randolph Churchill*.

 ©2001 The Teaching Company.

**Questions to Consider:**

1. Churchill once wrote, "It is said that famous men are usually the product of an unhappy childhood." Do you agree?

2. Why do you think Winston so admired his father? What lessons would you have learned from Lord Randolph's political career?

# Lecture Two—Transcript
## Young Churchill

In our last lecture we began to look at Winston Churchill through the image of his famous ancestor, John, the Duke of Marlborough. Now, Winston Churchill was greatly influenced by the career of Marlborough, and his attachment to Marlborough was more than ancestral pride. In Marlborough Churchill saw the fruition of an early period of English liberty—the Glorious Revolution of 1688, which had established the power of Parliament against the crown, and Marlborough was a parliamentary general. There was also the deep attachment that Churchill felt for truth, and he was deeply angered at the insults that had been hurled against Marlborough and continued to be hurled against Marlborough, and he wrote his biography of his ancestor in an effort to reverse these false statements. As we shall see, Winston Churchill himself, throughout his career, would be hounded by false accusations. He would be mistrusted, he would be called a political adventurer, even has John, the Duke of Marlborough, had been called a political adventurer.

There is also the notion of the ingratitude of democracy. Now, Marlborough did not live in an age of democracy, but Parliament tore him down despite all of his services. So, as we shall see, Winston Churchill, despite all of his services, would be given in his own terms the order of the boot by the British electorate in July of 1945. John, the Duke of Marlborough, fell from power, but he retained his title. He retained his palace at Blenheim. But his only son died young, and the Marlborough titles would pass down through his daughter, Anne, who married the Earl of Sunderland, Charles Spencer. The Churchill and Spencer name would be linked ever there after, Winston Spencer-Churchill. In fact, in this fashion, Winston Churchill and the late Princess Diana were related, and the coat of arms that flies over Blenheim Palace has both the Churchill and the Spencer arms in it—the griffin of the Spencer's and the lion of the Churchill's.

Now the descendents of the Duke of Marlborough did not distinguish themselves except for gambling, spending a great deal of money. One of them was forced to live just in a couple of rooms in the palace, that was all he could afford. But Churchill's grandfather began the restoration of the family reputation. He served well in Parliament and was Lord-Lieutenant of Ireland. Now Winston

©2001 The Teaching Company.

Churchill was never the Duke of Marlborough. His father, Lord Randolph, was the second son of the Duke of Marlborough. Lord Randolph was, from his earliest days (this is Churchill's father), an impetuous man; he made a very bad record at Oxford and his father was deeply concerned about him. But at the time when Churchill was born, November 30, 1874, Lord Randolph had been elected to Parliament and was beginning to make his mark as a speaker of great brilliance.

If Churchill were an English aristocrat on his father's side, on his mother's side Winston Churchill was an American, a full-blooded American. His mother was Jeanette Jerome; she was the daughter of a very wealthy New York financier, a self-made man who not only made a lot of money on the stock exchange, owned the *New York Times* for a period, but was also quite a sporting gentleman and liked to drive up and down the streets of New York in a fine carriage and owned many race horses and was part owner of a race track. He was one of the Americans of that period who made fortunes, lost them and made them again. He would give a dinner party which ladies would receive diamond bracelets as little favors, and he would spend seventy thousand dollars (in those days currency) giving those kinds of parties. His daughters were raised largely in Europe and spent a lot of time in England with their mother, and it was there, on August 12, 1873, that Jennie Jerome and her sisters were invited to a party on board a British ship in honor of the Czar-to-be of Russia and given by the Prince and Princess of Wales. So they went and she was introduced to Randolph Churchill and on the invitation she had written met Randolph. He was impetuous wooer as well. He wanted to go out with her the next day, and then the next day, and on the third day proposed marriage.

Well, her father thought it was a pretty good idea, but for the Duke of Marlborough, his father, this was the final blow. He is going to marry this American woman, and he writes his son and says you don't know what kind of trouble you are getting into. I have made some inquires about this father of her's. He is a sharp trader. He does not have a good reputation. He strikes me as one of these Americans of the most vulgar kind. But Randolph pursued and so his father said all right, if the father of this woman will make a generous monetary settlement. And Jennie's father and the Duke wrote back and forth until they agreed upon what seemed a reasonable settlement. But then, was it going to Randolph or was it going to go to the girl? And her father said it must go to her, that is how they do it in Russia. The Duke of Marlborough said we are in England and we are going to do it my way, it is going to Randolph. Well again, they split the difference, and in April 1874, the two were married. The Duke of Marlborough and his wife the Duchess did not come to the wedding. This was a very clear snub, but they were back in good feeling with their son and had invited them to Blenheim Palace in November.

Now, Jennie was seven months pregnant and she went out hunting and fell, and then when out on a pony ride over very rough ground, and then to everybody's amazement showed up that night at the ball and was dancing away when suddenly she realized she was going to have the baby. They started to rush her off to her bedroom, but they had to go through the library at Blenheim (which is probably the longest room in all of England) and so she couldn't make it, so they whisked her into a bedroom that was being used as a cloakroom. There she gave birth to young Winston. The first decision I made in life, he said, was to be born at Blenheim; I am most satisfied with that decision he said. He was always proud of his American heritage, he delighted in the fact that his mother had some Iroquois Indian in her background and that on her side he had several ancestors who fought in the army of George Washington as officers.

So, he was born, and at that moment his father was beginning his parliamentary career. Lord Randolph, a powerful man, huge swooping mustaches, rather protruding eyes, he set out to rise very, very fast in the Conservative party. He set out to rise by taking on the leadership. He set forth a program of Tory democracy in which he argued for education for the poor, health insurance, social security, pension plans, unemployment insurance. But at this very moment, as he was beginning to make his mark in Parliament, his speeches being very rapidly given, very forcefully given, a master of sarcasm, he showed his impetuosity. This is a tangled story of people long dead. But the gist of it is the Marquee of Blandford (that is to say, Lord Randolph's brother, all these English aristocrats had various titles at various times and before you get to be the Duke of Marlborough you are the Marquee of Blandford), the Marquee of Blandford was carrying on this affair with the wife of an Earl. Well, that was not unusual; after all, Winston's mother was said to have slept with 200 men; so there was nothing unusual about this. But the thing was they were not discreet. And while her husband was off in India with the Prince of Wales, as a matter of fact, she just eloped with Lord

    ©2001 The Teaching Company.

Randolph's brother, and they were living together openly. And she wrote her husband (this is even more indiscreet), saying I am leaving you, I love this man too much. So her husband came back immediately, took the children away and was going to turn her out on the street.

Well, it got more complicated because the brother of the seduced woman told the Marquee of Blandford he wanted a duel, but the Marquee didn't want a duel, so the brother said I am going to shoot you down on the street. It was really getting out of hand and so Lord Randolph decided he should take matters under control. And what did he do? He went to the Princess of Wales, and he said I have these letters showing that your husband sleeps with her as well. Now I want you to put a stop to all of this harassment. That is the most extraordinary thing in the world, of course Queen Victoria was told about, and it was a public scandal, which you could not have. Well, the shrewd, many-times Prime Minister, Disraeli, came up with a solution. Let the Duke of Marlborough go off as Lord-Lieutenant of Ireland, let Lord Randolph go with him as his private secretary, get the whole family out of England for a while, and it will come to a rest.

And so it would be that Winston's first memories were really of Ireland and living there in the palace of the Lord-Lieutenant of Ireland, his grandfather, and of his nurse, Mrs. Everest. She was never married, "Mrs." was just a courtesy title, but she loved him, she took care of him. These were not soccer moms in those days. Lady Randolph was not a soccer mom, she did not take Winston to choir practice and baseball and things of this sort. She rarely saw him, she might see him once a day if she were at home. He would brought in all cleaned and diapered by the nanny, by the lady Winston always called "Woom" (that is what he called Mrs. Everest) and she would show him to the mother. The mother would pat him and send him back to bed. His father would almost never see him. But Woom took care of him.

Winston described that perhaps his earliest memory was riding on a donkey with Woom, and they saw these soldiers. His nanny was convinced they were Irish terrorists and she shrieked, the donkey threw him off. I got a concussion, Winston said, and that was my introduction to Irish politics. But then some thing even gloomier came upon the horizon, a governess. So, I began my bout with education, Winston wrote. If you put letters together they made words, and reading wasn't that bad, but then came figures, mathematics, strange things. Why, these figures were always getting in debt with one another, and they borrowed from one another, and then they had to be paid back in some fashion. I never really mastered mathematics he said; once, once I saw as into an abyss with clarity the whole of mathematics, but it was after dinner and I let it go and never recaptured it. But he began his schooling, the family came back from Ireland and all was forgiven.

Lord Randolph began again his parliamentary career and made himself quite a name. In fact, it seems only a matter of time before he became Prime Minister. When the Conservative party was returned to power in 1885, Lord Randolph was made Chancellor of the Exchequer (a very early age for this powerful post, a post generally regarded as a stepping-stone to being Prime Minister), to be in charge of the treasury, like our Secretary of Treasury, above all charge for preparing the budget. And Lord Randolph set out to put himself in opposition to the Prime Minister, Lord Salisbury, taking positions opposite that of the Prime Minister, opposite of his boss, in other words, on almost every possible issue. And growing around him, a growingly strong group of fellow Conservative members, clearly planning a coup to overthrow Lord Salisbury.

Well, in December 1886, it came to a head over an issue of budget. Lord Randolph demanded that his budget be accepted, as it was, which entailed considerable cuts to the military budget. Lord Salisbury said no, that is not the budget that we want. That is not our policy. These cuts are inappropriate. So, Lord Randolph said, here, you have my resignation—again, the same kind of impetuosity that led him to go to the Princess of Wales. He thought he was indispensable—he was not—Lord Salisbury said I accept it with delight. And then Churchill thought that all of his friends in Parliament would flock to his side, but no, they were as he said, rats leaving the sinking ship. And there he was removed from the Exchequer. When Lord Salisbury was asked, aren't you going to bring Lord Randolph back in some position? He said have you ever heard of somebody with a boil on their neck who wanted it back? Sure enough, Lord Randolph's power began to decline rapidly and with it his physical health.

The standard view still today is that he suffered from syphilis that he had contracted as a young man and that grew rapidly worse. What his doctors diagnosed as a general paralysis, and this is what Lady Randolph was told, Winston's mother, that she should avoid contact with her husband in that fashion. But in the meantime, there was Winston to raise. At the age of seven he had been sent off to boarding school. Now, he adored his father and worshipped his mother; she was like the evening star, he said, for me. She was a beautiful woman, dark haired, piercing eyes, a beautiful figure, but he saw little of his parents. At the age of seven he was sent to his first boarding school, St. George's, a very fine boarding school that is supposed to prepared you for Eton College, the best private school in England, what the British call a public school. He describes that first encounter with public school education.

The headmaster came in and put a greenish brown book into my hand and opened it. He said, "Here, this the first declension of the Latin noun, mensa. I will come back in thirty minutes to see if you have learned it." Well, he came back in thirty minutes, and I said, "Mensa, Mensae, Mensam, Mensa, Mensa." He said, "Wonderful, boy. You shall do just fine." "Sir?" "Yes." "There are three words that say mensa." "Yes." "Well, why are there three mensas?" "Well, this mensa is table." "I see." "And this mensa, it is O table." "Sir? Oh table? Why would I say O table, sir?" For I was generally curious, Winston wrote later, "O table. "You use it in addressing a chair, and it is an invocation. If you are speaking to a table it is what you use." "But sir, I almost never do, fact, I never have." "You are being impudent. Well, do that again and you will be beaten, and beaten most severely," He [Churchill] said that was my introduction to the classics, from which I understand so many of our most famous men had gained so much pleasure and profit.

And he was not good at school; there is no question about it. Lady Randolph, in the midst of her busy social calendar, had to constantly read these reports from the headmaster. Winston is the worst in his class, he is slovenly, he is greedy at the table, he eats too much, and his manners are terrible. He seems unable to learn anything. He was a naughty boy, a troublesome boy, and he was punished severely. He said, "The standard of punishment there at St. George's would not have been permitted these years later in any of our reformatories of today. You were dragged into a room off the library and beaten until the blood came out." Two years after being treated in such a way, while he was home on vacation, Woom saw the welts, the beatings on his back, and she told Lady Randolph. He was taken out of that school and put in, he said, to a much kinder school in Brighton, the seaside resort run by two ladies. They were not nearly so brutal, and they let him learn some things he thought were kind of interesting like history, French; there was still that terrible Latin; and they were even talking about Greek, but he would later proudly say no one ever made me write a Latin verse, and I never learned Greek beyond the alphabet.

And there were still the reports that he just wasn't any good at school, he just didn't pay attention, he didn't do his reports, and more than that, he was lonely. He made no friends in school. His mother would almost never come to visit him; she forgot his Christmas presents. His father was never quite sure how old he was. Lord Randolph came to Brighton when Winston around eleven and gave a speech, and Winston writes his father and says, Papa, why didn't you come to see me? You were just across the street from our school. Then he wrote, Papa, I see that you are giving another speech in Brighton, may I come? No answer, no visit. Papa, I see that you could catch this later train and just come see me? No answer, no visit. Once his father said after he had shouted to Winston (Winston was making noise when the father was at home on one of Winston's vacations), he shouted at him, and seeing how upset Winston was, his father said, you must forgive me, boy, older people have much on their mind and sometimes they are not as thoughtful as they should be. That was the only moment of intimacy I ever had with my father.

And then off to Harrow. Eaton was the great "public" school. It was where his father had gone to public school; it was the preparatory for the Christ Church College at Oxford. But his father wouldn't let him go to Eaton. You will just embarrass me there, you are such a stupid boy. And so he was sent to Harrow, a good public school, but not Eaton, thought to be in a more healthy part of England. There he began another bout with education. The headmaster tried to be kind to him, took him under his wing, even gave him special tutoring in Latin, but it went nowhere. He just could not learn Latin and didn't want to learn Latin. He was supposed to do better in French, but what he really liked was English. He remembered fondly his master in English, Mr. Somervell. Now, he said:

He would take apart for us an English sentence. He would use different colors of ink to show what was the noun and the verb and the adjectives. And he got into our fiber the structure of an English sentence. Now that is a noble thing. Let boys learn Latin if they want to, let them even learn Greek, but I would never flog a boy for not knowing Latin or Greek, but I would flog him and flog him hard for not knowing English that is his language. And I often noted that those of my contemporaries who had been so well versed in Greek and Latin perhaps had less success that I did lagging their own tongue, English.

He liked history, and his father was notified by the mother in one of the letters that Winston seems to be doing better in history, he is still doing bad in almost every thing. In fact he is so irregular that he is almost regular in his irregularity. He is late for every thing and of course the most depressing thing of all was parents' day. His parents, of course, never came, but other boys' parents were there, and they always marched out in the academic order, the best student in the class going out first. And here was Winston, always last. The people would almost invariably say, look, Randolph's boy is the last of all because Randolph had so many enemies, and there was little Winston trudging out there in his top hat last of all.

But, Lord Randolph heard that he was doing a little better in history, so he came in one day when Winston was there on vacation and said, tell me what the Grand Remonstrance was, a significant fact about the reign of King Charles. And Winston said, the Grand Remonstrance, Papa? Yes! They tell me you are a history scholar. When Parliament took away the king's power and cut off his head. Damn little idiot. But, Papa, that seems to me the Grandest Remonstrance of all. Then one day his father came in, Winston was home on vacation again, and Winston had 1,500 toy soldiers, and they were laid out in magnificent array. His father came in and studied them for about 20 minutes, and then said, boy, would you like to be a soldier? Yes, Papa, I would like to be a soldier.

And so he was removed from the academic class, what we might call the college preparatory track, and put into the army class, which was for all the adults in the school. So, he did not have to learn any more Greek, no more Latin, and he did a little better. He said with that one snap decision by my father, my career seemed to have been set. But I used to for years think that he had seen in me some military genius. I later heard he simply thought I was too stupid to become a lawyer and thought I could only be a soldier. So, he plodded on through Harrow, finally graduated at almost the very bottom of the class and took his entrance examinations to Sandhurst, the great military college, and failed. Now his father was upset, but said, alright, you'll try again. But he failed again, and his father said, I am putting that boy into the business world, I am going to make a stockbroker out of him. One of the father's friends said, I know of this tutor who tutors boys just for getting them into Sandhurst, why don't you give Winston one more chance. So he had this tutor and the tutor kept writing the father and said, I do not wish you to be under false assumptions, I do not see how he can pass, I have never had a harder charge in my life. I do not think he is stupid, in fact, at times he gives me a sense of being truly bright, but his absolute lack of discipline, his irregularity, his desire to learn only the things that he wants to learn is, I think, an insurmountable barrier.

But he took the exam and got in. He wrote his father this most joyful letter, how proud he was. He got back this letter, you are a constant disappointment to me, there are various ways of passing an examination and you choose always the worst. Your performance is slovenly. I have learned that you will not be allowed into the infantry class, you must be in the cavalry class, and now in addition to everything else, I must pay for a horse while you are there. Let me tell you something, not only are you a complete failure, you are the worst sort of failure, because you have these enormous pretenses about your ability. I see nothing ahead of you but failure. You will be a wastrel of the kind that decorates the fringes of society. Do not write me any more, I do not wish to hear anything more from you.

But Sandhurst was different than Harrow, you got to learn things that were interesting. Churchill, like John Dewey, thought perhaps you should teach children by getting them interesting in things, not forcing them to learn Latin, but letting them study things that interested them and then go on to something else and ever deeper into a subject. And he said, there at Sandhurst, we study things that had an immediate value, we study tactics and fortifications. We studied typography, we have studied military law and military administration, all of which I was going to be using very soon, and the course only lasted 18 months. So you progressed rapidly, and you had a great deal of free time, I was frequently invited to the officer's

 ©2001 The Teaching Company.

mess at fine regiments, and so what it was to be a soldier and so I progressed. In fact, in the class of 130, he graduated twentieth. So he could do the work, it was just that no one had bothered to interest him.

In the meantime, his father's health declined evermore rapidly. His speeches in Parliament were pathetic to hear; he could no longer keep the thread of his ideas going. He started off with a trip around the world, and shortly before he left, he wrote another searing letter to Winston. I just went to my watchmaker's to have my watch oiled before I leave, he showed me the watch that I gave you when you did well that first term at Sandhurst, a beautiful watch. It is rusted and he says it will have to be completely taken apart, I will never give you anything else. And Churchill wrote back, but Papa you don't understand. We don't have a real pocket and it popped out of the slip where I carry it, and it fell into a stream and I dove down into the stream and I could not find it. So I got permission to take some soldiers that are there on the base and we dammed up the stream and diverted it and made it dry. I got it out. I just didn't want to make you mad by telling you about it, but I will pay for it. But when the watch was repaired, Lord Randolph gave it to Churchill's younger brother who kept it for the rest of his life. Lord Randolph could not complete the trip around the world, he had to be brought back in a straightjacket and died in lingering pain and agony, the same year that Churchill would pass out of Sandhurst.

Churchill wrote that the solitary tree, if it grows at all, grows to be strong and sturdy, and frequently, a boy deprived of a father's love feels determined to win back that love even after the father is gone. Churchill would spend a part of his life trying to live up to the expectations of the father who denied him that love. The years from 20 to 25, Churchill said that is the greatest time of life, and to that time in Churchill's life we will turn in our next lecture.

# Lecture Three
# On the Empire's Frontier

**Scope:**

As a young officer on the northwest frontier of India, Churchill displayed the courage, ambition, and boldness of spirit that was his hallmark throughout his long life. We follow Churchill as he rides in the last great cavalry charge at the Battle of Omdurman in 1898. We are with Churchill in South Africa during the Boer War as his intrepid spirit makes him a national celebrity. We come back to Britain with him as he wins his seat in Parliament in 1900. By the age of 26, Churchill was a member of Parliament and a best-selling author and had made himself a millionaire through his writings.

## Outline

I.   After Sandhurst, Churchill received a commission in a famous regiment, the Fourth Hussars.

   A.  In 1895, he was posted in India, the jewel in the crown of the British Empire.

   B.  At that time, Britain ruled an empire 91 times its size (the size of the State of Colorado).

   C.  Churchill believed the British Empire to be a force for good, bringing law and civilization all over the globe, raising up men and women in a civilization of a bright new age.

   D.  Typically, Churchill wanted to make good use of his time until he was due to leave for India.

   1.  He went, as a newspaper correspondent, to Cuba, where rebels were fighting for their freedom against the Spanish.

   2.  He described the action, published his opinions, and proved himself to be calm under fire.

   3.  When he returned to New York, he found himself in a controversy.

   4.  The press questioned his presence in Cuba and his alleged support for Spanish colonial rule.

   5.  Controversy would dog Churchill throughout his life.

   E.  Back in England, he defended the freedom of prostitutes and argued that the true solution to social problems lay in education and improvements to social conditions, as opposed to prudish censorship.

    **F.** Churchill described himself as a "passive conformist in religion."

**II.** He served with distinction and bravery on the northwest frontier in the Malakand campaign of 1897, when Afghan tribesmen rebelled against British rule.

    **A.** In Afghanistan, he also reported on the campaign as a war correspondent.

    **B.** He published a book about the Malakand campaign, which became a bestseller.

        **1.** In it, he showed courage by criticizing British strategy in the campaign.

        **2.** In doing so, he aroused the anger of the War Office and Lord Kitchener in particular.

        **3.** His book won the praise of Lord Salisbury, who offered his support.

        **4.** Churchill asked Salisbury to help him join Lord Kitchener in the Sudanese campaign in 1898.

    **C.** He served with equal distinction in this campaign against Sudanese tribesmen, which culminated in the Battle of Omdurman on September 2, 1898.

    **D.** Again, he served as a war correspondent.

    **E.** He criticized the squalor of war, including Kitchener's brutality to the enemy, his cruelty to prisoners, and his destruction of the tomb of the Sudanese religious leader.

    **F.** Again, Churchill's book about the campaign was highly successful.

**III.** Churchill resigned his commission in the British army and went to South Africa.

    **A.** In 1899–1902, the Boer, or South African, War was the struggle against British rule in South Africa, waged by the Boers (Afrikaners, descendants of Dutch settlers).

    **B.** Churchill served as a war correspondent (1899–1900).

    **C.** On November 15, 1899, not quite 25 years old, Churchill joined an expeditionary force and wound up as a prisoner of the Boers in Pretoria.

1. He eventually made a dramatic escape to Portuguese East Africa.
2. His flight to freedom made him a national celebrity in England.

    **D.** He wrote two books based on his South African experiences, which became bestsellers.

**IV.** Back in England, Churchill entered politics.

    **A.** He was elected to Parliament as a member of the Conservative Party from Oldham in 1900.

    **B.** At the age of 26, Churchill was a war hero, a best-selling author, and a member of Parliament and, by his writing and lectures, had made himself a millionaire.

**Essential Reading:**

Manchester, *Churchill*, volume I, pp. 210–335.

**Supplementary Reading:**

Churchill, *My Early Life*, pp. 61–370.

Sandys, *Churchill*.

**Questions to Consider:**

1. Would you agree that Churchill succeeded in spite of, rather than because of, the education system he encountered?

2. In later years, when Churchill had to send men to their deaths in war, no one could question his military service and personal bravery. Do you think this factor is important in a wartime leader?

# Lecture Three—Transcript
# On the Empire's Frontier

In our last lecture, we looked at the childhood of Winston Churchill. The difficult childhood of "a troublesome boy" as he was called. His distant relationships with his parents who seemed to have little time for him, and his struggles with a school system that was determined to force him into a mold, rather than recognizing the abilities that were already there. It was only when he went to military academy, a choice made by his father in a snap decision, only at Sandhurst that Churchill began to find himself in school to study subjects he enjoyed and to make a quite good record. After having passed out of Sandhurst, he was offered a commission as a Second Lieutenant in the Fourth Hussars, one of the finest regiments in the British army. And he would soon be posted out to India at the very height of the British Empire.

The British Empire, spoken in 1900, it meant a nation, it was a great and mighty power ruled from Britain. The empire, in the First World War, men died for God, king and empire. And Winston Churchill would tell his brother, Jack, I want to devote my life to the service of this empire I love so well. Queen Victoria ruled over an empire 91 times larger than Britain itself. Britain is the size of Colorado, and that small empire, that small nation ruled a series of islands, almost whole continents. India was the jewel in the crown of the empire, but it stretched from Canada out to Fiji. It included almost the entire center part of Africa, from Cape to Cairo you could go on a railroad staying the entire time in British territory. "Land of hope and glory, mother of the free/How can we extol thee, we who are born of thee?/Wide are thou boundaries and wider yet shall they be set/God, who made thee mighty, make thee mightier yet." Such was a hymn that would remain one of Churchill's favorite songs all through his life. This grand, vast empire which he and so many believed to be a force for good, bringing law and civilization all across the globe, raising up not in our terms but in the terms of those days, raising up men and women into a civilization and a bright new age. The empire of Britain, and Churchill would be a central figure in that empire, until its final demise.

He was not yet 21 and he had a brief time before he had to go out to India, and he chose to make the best use of it—very typical of Churchill. Not sitting around honing, playing cards the way most of his fellow officers did. He wanted to go to Cuba; he wanted to see some real action. He wanted to make a name of himself, and so he made use of one of his father's old friends who was the British diplomat in Madrid. He got papers of introduction to the Spanish government in Cuba, which at that very moment was trying to put down a revolt. And he also managed to get a contract as a newspaper correspondent to send back dispatches and be paid for them. Quite an enterprising young man. He sailed off in early November of 1895 with one of his friends from the army. They went first to New York where he stayed in the apartment of a considerable American politician, Bourke Cochran, who was also alleged to be have been one of the paramours of his mother, and he gave Churchill an introduction into democratic politics. Churchill vastly admired Bourke Cochran's ability as a speaker. Then Churchill went off to Cuba, and there, on his 21$^{st}$ birthday, November 30, he came under fire.

When they had arrived in Havana, the expedition which was going to punish the rebels in the interior had already left, and so Churchill took off by train and by boat, caught up with them within four days and was there when the first action started. He described the bullets sailing over his head and then, in the midst of all of this, the Spanish forces took a siesta, ate a huge breakfast, the rebels seem to have done the same. They went to sleep in the middle of the afternoon, and the rebels started firing sooner, they woke up sooner, began firing again. And Churchill said once again the bullets came crashing through our tent, but I noticed that the man hanging in front of me, and the direction from which the bullets came, was a substantial figure, fat, in other words, and I figured the bullets would have to come through him before they got me so I closed my eyes again, calmness under fire, and without ever drawing his pistol.

Nonetheless, he was there with the troops as they fought and formed some ideas about the conflict. Yes, the rebels were right to fight for their freedom. But would they use it well? And he saw that the Spaniards looked upon their empire the way the British did, they did not want to give it up but make it worthy, he said in his dispatches, make it worthy of an empire. Then he came back to New York and immediately found himself in a controversy. Controversy followed Churchill his entire life; there were always plenty of people who hated him, told untruths about him, who were eager to slander him. And already this 21-year-old, very unprepossessing soldier in the army, found American papers attacking him. They wanted to know why he had been in Cuba. Support for the rebels was very strong. Why had he been in Cuba? He said I didn't even draw my revolver. Then the English newspapers took it up and said he ought to be withdrawn from the service for this kind of activity. There he was in controversy and defended himself in his first press conference, and then sailed back to England and was soon posted out to India. Controversy: Churchill never, never avoided it.

While in England, he gave his first public speech. Ladies of the empire, he said, I stand for freedom. While the ladies were ladies of the night and the empire was the Empire Theatre. The Empire Theatre was at the center of a number of bars, and these ladies of the night used to parade up and down in front of the bars making all kinds of propositions. A group of outraged citizens demanded that a wall be put up so they could not walk in front of the bars. Churchill went and made this speech; he encouraged a group to tear down that wall. And then wrote an article in the newspapers and said the true solution for social problems lies in education and improving the social climate, making people better off. It does not lie in a bunch of prudes censoring the actions of other people, actions that harm no one—so from the very outset, the idea of individual freedom and a rejection of regimentation, of censorship. In fact, he was never a very religious man. He was a "passive conformist" he said. He never took religion very seriously; he believed perhaps in a stronger force, but above all we make our own destiny.

So, he was determined to make his own destiny when he went to India to take up his position with the Fourth Hussars. British regiments had a history of their own and the Fourth Hussars was one of the most distinguished in the British army. In those days you were expected to have a considerable income of your own to be an officer. You were expected, in a cavalry regiment, to keep a polo pony. Churchill would have several servants when he went out to India. But what he wanted above all was action and the Fourth Hussars were not going into action. But other regiments were going into action on the northwest frontier, the Khyber Pass, a place Americans have come to know something about in recent days. Going up against Afghan tribesmen and Churchill used all of his influence, asking again and again if he could not be detached to join the regiments going into action there, the Bengal Lancers. And not only did he get permission, but he also arranged with the paper in London to write newspaper dispatches again. His dispatches coming back from Cuba had been very well received, so he got permission to write more newspaper dispatches, and then, which was highly unusual, got permission as a soldier while also being a war correspondent.

So there he was out at the northwest frontier, with those tribesman who valued their independence above all else, who lived in their own individual castles made of mud brick, who all carried rifles, and who hated the idea of the British infringing on that freedom. And Britain was equally determined to bring that area of India under ever closer control. The Afghans fought again and again. And again and again, the British sent regiments to pacify them. So the Bengal Lancers found themselves going up the valley called the Malakand River Valley and Churchill was with them. Churchill was detached to a small group of some 85 men, 8 British officers and the rest Indian troops who made their way up to a height to reconnoiter, when suddenly, he writes, "the whole hillside exploded into white puffs and the Afghans were upon us. One of my men turned around and faced me, his entire eye shot out, men began to drop, and the Afghans were upon them, beginning to horribly mutilate them." And Churchill picked up a rifle, and firing into the enemy dropped one, then two, then three, then the Agitant came up and said, we better make our way back down, only to be suddenly shot in the knee himself. Churchill helped carry his body down and helped rescue other men. Then suddenly, an Afghan was upon him again, and he pulled out his pistol and shot him dead. So, there, seeing his first action as a British officer, he was praised for valor, courage and his resolute spirit mentioned in the dispatches. That was quite an honor, specifically being noted that he did not have to be there at all, that he had asked for this service. And so there, on the northwest frontier and on further actions riding his little gray pony up and down the skirmish lines, he first marked himself out for that personal courage.

No one ever doubted his personal courage, whether it was on the field of battle, in Parliament, or facing Hitler. And later on, when he had to send men to their deaths in battle, no one could say that he had tried to dodge a draft; he was a soldier. Having served on the northwest frontier, he came back to London for a while on leave and took the dispatches that he had written for the newspaper and turned them into his first book, *The Malakand Field Force*. It became a very good seller. He turned it out in a few months, and again showing his

©2001 The Teaching Company.

courage by not hesitating to criticize. You see, a man careful of his career would have said only good things about the British force. Churchill questioned the leadership; he questioned the role of the political office in trying to negotiate with the tribesmen instead of fighting with them; and he also questioned the very supplies that were brought to the British troops. He aroused the anger of the war office and, in particular, a man becoming one of the most important of all British soldiers, the man who would come to be known as Lord Kitchener, Horatio Kitchener.

But politicians elsewhere took note of the book, and while he was back in London, after the book had come out, he received a note from the private secretary of the Prime Minister, Lord Salisbury, the same man who had been responsible for his father's fall. He asked if young Churchill would call upon him. And he showed me in with Old World courtesy, asked me to sit upon a sofa, and for 20 minutes talked to me about my book. I have learned more from your book about what is going on in the northwest frontier than all the dispatches that come into Parliament. Having been praised, I started to get up, but he motioned me back down and spoke on and said, I want also for you to know how much you remind me of your father with whom I passed so many days and worked together on so many important projects. If there is ever any thing I can do for you, let me know. Well, Churchill knew exactly what he wanted Lord Salisbury to do for him, he wanted to be able to go take part in the great expedition that was moving up the Nile. So he wrote a little note back to the private secretary, and said, I hope you don't think me forward, but I took Lord Salisbury at his word, is there a way you can get me detached from the Fourth Hussars who are in India to join the expedition going up the Nile? And so the private secretary wrote to Lord Kitchener, who was in charge of the expedition, and he wrote back and said no, under no circumstances will I have him with me. I will not have an officer who is critical of authority; he is a military adventurer, an opportunist. I will take with me only men who are sound. Well, Churchill wrote again, could you try one more time, and finally Lord Kitchener, with very bad grace, gave in and Churchill found himself again detached from the Fourth Hussars, going up river and taking part in this grand campaign attached to one of the Lancer Divisions, the 21st Lancers.

Once again, he got a contract from the newspapers to write dispatches. His *Malakand Field Force* had done well and the newspapers were willing to give him another contract. So 1,400 miles up the Nile they went. It was again a struggle against Islamic forces, in this case, the Sudanese. More than a decade before, the whole of the Sudan has risen up under a magnificent charismatic leader, the Mahdi, the savior, a man who was in the grip of a vision that a united Islam would overthrow all the decadent forces of the west. I see myself, he said, praying in the great mosque of Khartoum, I see myself praying in the great mosque at Cairo. I see myself praying in the great mosque at Mecca, I see myself praying in the great mosque at Jerusalem. And his troops went into battle thinking they could not be pierced by bullets. In an effort to stem the tide, the British had sent out one of the most famous generals of his day, Charles "Chinese" Gordon, and he had failed, Khartoum had been captured. He himself had been slain in 1885, and this lay like blot upon the honor of Britain.

So now, 13 years later, this mighty expeditionary force of 20,000 British troops and thousands of Egyptian troops marched into the Sudan against the successor of the Madhi, the Khalifa. It was with these troops that Churchill marched along. At one point, he had task of getting the supplies ready, and when he had finished, it was late in the evening, so he crossed the river to try to catch up with the rest of his regiment and found that they had gone on ahead. He was told to go down the river, follow it along, and he would come upon them. He started off and found the river, turned quite a bit, and it was suddenly dark. He tried to guide himself by the stars, but clouds came up and there he was alone. He spent the night uncomfortably and in the morning found an Arab who, of course, could not speak English. Churchill did not know Arabic, and Churchill rubbed his tummy as though he were hungry, nothing happen. He said, *baksheesh*, (tip or money), the Arab went off and got him food, fed his horse, and then showed him where the Lancers were. So he began to move out with them.

His commanding officers sent him on ahead and said, see if you can discern where the army is. Churchill came over a hill and saw them there; he writes "This is how the crusades must have been." Many of the Sudanese wore chain mail armor, carrying spears and swords— magnificent figures as the sun glinted off of them. Churchill rode back and was sent on to Kitchener, whom he had never really met. He rode up to Kitchener, and Kitchener, not knowing really who he was, and Churchill simply gave Kitchener the word: The army of the enemy is within sight. Kitchener said, then let them come on, we'll fight them today, as well as tomorrow, it doesn't matter. (He is a soldier.) Now he described Kitchener to his mother as a brutal kind of man, but a soldier.

The next day, September 2, 1898, that the battle would be joined. The Lancers had as their task to turn the flank of the enemy force. And as they marched towards the enemy, thinking that the enemy was armed only with spears, the "Dervishes" as the British called them, stood up and began to fire. "Wheel right and then gallop and charge," and Churchill led his men into the very center of the enemy force. He had hurt his arm in an accident and so could not use a saber, so he pulled out his pistol, a ripper, as he called it, and began to fire into the enemy. It was two minutes of total concentration, that was all. But men falling and dying, Churchill shooting at least five men, until the enemy force broke, and then it was over. First there was the exhilaration, and indeed, the complete victory over the foe, and then the scene of the battle caught Churchill, obsessed him— men lying there in pain, the flies, the screaming horses—war, he said, is glorious, but also squawked, beware of drinking the cup of glory to its dregs because you will find them bitter.

He criticized Kitchener in his newspaper dispatches, criticized him for brutality to the enemy, for cruelty to prisoners, and for destroying the tomb of the Madhi, a religious leader. He made no friend of Kitchener, and they would meet again at a critical moment in Churchill's career. But his book, *The River War*, was another bestseller. He came back to London on leave and found himself becoming quite a well-known author. There was a Winston Churchill in America, an American author who wrote novels. He started up a correspondence with Winston Churchill, and said, I like your books and I hope you like mine, I am sending you some. I shall put down, from now on, on the cover of my novels, Winston Churchill, American, so people will not confuse us.

And then there was more action. Churchill, by this time, was resigning his commission in the army, but he wanted to go out to South Africa. He wanted to go out to where the Boer War had begun, the South African War, in some ways the first war of the twentieth century that looked forward, in a way, to the bloody struggles on the Western Front of 1914. It was a war of liberation fought by the sturdy Dutch farmers of South Africa against British rule. It was a threat to the empire, it was war of extremes, a war that was both chivalrous and cruel, and Churchill wanted to be part of it. So he went out as a newspaper correspondent, without an army commission, landed in South Africa and wanted to get as quickly as possible to the front. So, he took a boat, took a train, and still found that he could not get to the front itself.

The town of Ladysmith was surrounded by Boers, was under a siege, and he was stuck there, in a British camp. But he met an old friend from Indian days, and Captain Haldane agreed to take Churchill along with him in an armored car, going out to probe the lines of the Boers. So, Churchill, with a number of troops, got on board this armored car. It was November 15, 1899 (he was still not 25 years of age), and they went along and came up over a ridge when suddenly they saw a mass of the Boer army, these Dutch farmers, in many ways, were like the Confederates in our own civil war, fighting with bravery, fighting with determination against a far better equipped army. But the Boers had artillery as well; they were getting help from Germany and Holland. They had heavy artillery, and suddenly, they opened up upon the armored car. With this heavy artillery blasting down upon it, the armored car started going back in reverse, when suddenly there was an enormous clanging roar and the car went off the tracks. The Boers had put heavy boulders across the track and knocked it off.

Churchill volunteered to go up and see if he could get the car back up on the tracks. So he raced up to the engineer who was shouting, I am getting out of here, they don't pay me to get shot at, they pay me to drive trains. And Churchill said, buck up, nobody is ever shot twice in the same battle. You are wounded a little bit now, but you will be okay. Besides, I am going to get you a medal for this. So he got the engineer to work with him, and they worked back and forth for more than 70 minutes trying to get some of the cars back up on the track. Churchill being under fire the entire time. In his effort to get the train on the track, he ripped off his pistol, ripped off his field glasses, so he could have more maneuverability, and suddenly they got the cars going and Churchill rushed back, loaded wounded men on the cars, still under fire, and a portion of them went off. But there were still men under fire, other British troops, and Churchill came back and was trying to get them loaded, when suddenly, the Boers broke down upon them and the whole group began to disperse.

 ©2001 The Teaching Company.

Churchill was moving down towards the ravine, trying to avoid capture, when one of the Boers leveled his rifle at him and said, stop, halt. Churchill reached down for his pistol, but it wasn't there, he had tossed it away. So, Napoleon said when you are completely overwhelmed, surrender is a reasonable option. Churchill surrendered, was marched to prison in Pretoria and put into a school that had been turned into a prison. It was, he said, the most miserable experience of my time. His comments just ring with the humiliation and anger he felt at captivity. He also was assiduous in his attempts to get out. He kept writing to the Boer authority, saying, I am a war correspondent, I am not a soldier, you can't keep me as a prisoner of war. The Boer authorities write back and said, then why do the newspapers celebrate you as a hero under fire at the armored car? No, sir, you are a soldier and you are going to stay there. He would write again; they would write back. He was determined to get out of that prison.

The friend who had invited him along, Captain Haldane, was also there with him. They developed a bold plan to get out. They and one more soldier were going to escape through a latrine. There was a latrine that opened onto a back wall, so they laid their plans for December 12. But the first of them went out and came back; he said it is impossible, they are watching us too carefully. Churchill then went to the latrine, climbed up to where he could see the wall and just at that moment one of the Boer guards turned to another for a light for his cigarette and Churchill left out. But the others never came, and so there he was outside the wall, with very little cover. To go back and surrender himself would of course betray the whole plot.

So he simply walked off on his own. Walked through the streets of Pretoria, knowing no Dutch, where everybody was on the lookout for English spies. He put his hands in his pockets, whistled, finally got to a railroad yard, and took a train out. But, as he rode along on the train, he realized he didn't know which way he was going. What he wanted to do was go to the east, to Portuguese East Africa. But he didn't know where he was, so he jumped off, spent a day hungry with his only companion, he said, a vulture, who took a tremendous interest in his activities.

Then, as night came, he saw a light. He thought it might be an African village, and he knew that they hated the Boers, but he went and saw it was a regular house in the midst of mining area. He knocked on the door and a voice cried out, *wer ist da.* And Churchill said in English, I am a Dutchman, I have fallen off the train and hurt myself, I need help. The door opened, a man led him in, locked the door and said in English this time, tell me more. I think I had better tell you the truth, I am Winston Churchill, I am a war correspondent. And the man, John Howard, put out his hand and said, thank God you have come here. This is the only place you would have been safe for twenty miles. He hid Churchill and then got him on a train, arranged for help as Churchill went along on the train. Churchill sunk down in between bales of wool, being stalked at each station along the way. But the friend who had gone along with him bribed each of the railroad guards not to check his bales too carefully. So Churchill finally looked out and saw, in Portuguese, a station sign and knew he had made it to Portuguese East Africa. He fired off the pistol he had two times in joy and made his way to the capital of Portuguese East Africa.

When he got out, he walked immediately to the British consulate, and his heart soared when he saw the Union Jack flying there. He shouted out, I am here. A servant came and said, yes, you are here, so? And he said, well, I want to see the consul. I am sorry he is busy. Churchill stepped back and shouted out even more loudly, I am Winston-bloody-Churchill. The consul came down and said, do you know that you are famous? For the story had been picked up by the newspapers of his flight from prison, at a time when the British arms were suffering defeat, it was the one positive story.

So from Cape Town to London, Winston Churchill was a hero. This time he came back to London and ran for Parliament and was elected. He wrote two books based on his experience in South Africa; they too were best sellers. At the age of 26, this boy who was so troublesome, this boy who was such a failure in school, this wastrel, as his father called him, was a war hero, a best-selling author, a member of Parliament, and by his own writings and lectures had made himself, in today's currency, a millionaire. Now, I think that is quite an achievement in those years, which Churchill called the best that life has to offer. But life was just beginning for him, and to his early years in Parliament we'll turn in our next lecture.

©2001 The Teaching Company.

# Lecture Four
## Political Beginnings

**Scope:**

Churchill's political career rested on a bedrock of principles, which made him incomprehensible to run-of-the mill politicians. Accordingly, he never lacked for critics. However, his political acumen, his administrative abilities, and his brilliance as an orator carried him very far, very fast. When World War I began in 1914, Churchill was First Lord of the Admiralty, in charge of the British navy. He brought the navy to its peak of efficiency. However, his bedrock of principles led him to challenge the patently unsuccessful strategy of the British High Command. The result was the Dardanelles campaign of 1915.

## Outline

I. Churchill succeeded in becoming a war hero and best-selling author out of ambition and a need for recognition, fostered by his parents' neglect of him, his desire to prove himself to his father, and later, his desire to vindicate his father's memory.

    **A.** Churchill hoped to use his success as a soldier and author to boost his political career.

    **B.** In India, he had begun to educate himself by reading books that his mother sent him.

    **C.** His literary and speaking style were the product of having read a few books and having read them well.

    **D.** Edward Gibbon's (1737–1794) *The Decline and Fall of the Roman Empire* and Thomas Babington Macaulay's (1800–1859) histories, essays, and poetry were most influential on Churchill's style and approach to history.

    **E.** He also studied Parliamentary debates and his father's speeches.

    **F.** By the time he was writing about his adventures in South Africa, he had become a master of English prose.

    **G.** He believed that to become a truly great speaker you must believe in what you are saying.

    **H.** He wrote his own speeches.

**I.** Although each speech took him eight to 10 hours to prepare, people thought the speeches were extemporaneous.

**II.** When Churchill was first elected to Parliament, in 1900, Queen Victoria was nearing the end of her long reign (1837–1901), the British Empire was at its height, and Great Britain was the leading economic power in the world.

    **A.** There were also serious problems at home and abroad.

        **1.** An enormous gulf existed between rich and poor in Britain.

        **2.** Britain saw severe labor unrest.

        **3.** The issue of the status of Ireland caused violent agitation.

        **4.** The growing military might of Germany posed a threat.

    **B.** In the British system of government in 1911, Parliament, comprising the Crown, the House of Lords, and the House of Commons, was sovereign. This is the legal definition. The House of Commons was, and is, in fact, the sovereign body.

    **C.** The House of Lords could, at that time, veto legislation passed by the House of Commons.

    **D.** Britain was, and is, a Parliamentary democracy.

        **1.** There is no direct vote for the Prime Minister; the winning political party chooses its Prime Minister.

        **2.** Although each member of Parliament represents a geographical district, members do not have to reside in their districts.

    **E.** In 1900, there were two leading parties.

        **1.** Conservatives were more traditional in their values.

        **2.** Liberals believed that the government should play a bigger role in carrying out social programs.

**III.** Churchill, like his father, believed in a Tory democracy with a liberal cast, which would take care of its poor with various social programs, including education, health insurance, unemployment benefits, and recognition of trade unions.

    **A.** Although elected as a member of the Conservative Party, Churchill had a deep distrust of Conservative leaders, because they had been responsible for destroying his father's career.

**B.** By 1906, he had published a biography of his father in an effort to vindicate his father's memory.

**C.** For Churchill, Lord Randolph represented an England that was above petty partisanship.

**D.** However, his father's memory was not an asset to Churchill during these years.

**E.** Churchill's first speech in Parliament was controversial. He praised the Boers for fighting the war with bravery.

**F.** He was accused of trying to run imperialism on the cheap when he voted against large amounts of money being granted to the army.

**G.** He warned against trying to fight a war against Germany, because he believed Britain could never raise a large enough army to defeat the Germans.

**H.** He cautioned that the next war would be protracted and extremely costly in terms of lives and money.

**IV.** In 1904, Churchill decided to leave the Conservative Party, because the Conservatives were pushing a policy of tariffs, and Churchill believed in free trade.

**A.** He became a member of the Liberal Party.

**B.** His Conservative opponents called him a political opportunist; for the same reason, he also did not gain the full support of the Liberal Party.

**V.** In 1905, he was named Undersecretary of State for Colonies and was immediately assigned a controversial task: to develop a constitution for South Africa in the wake of the Boer War.

**A.** The constitution he developed was a key example of his spirit of magnanimity. It advocated a policy of "one man one vote" for the Boers and allowed them to keep their language.

**B.** The constitution he established would guide South Africa through World War II and tie it deeply to the British Empire.

**VI.** In 1908, he was appointed President of the Board of Trade, bringing him into the Cabinet and giving him the scope for his program of social reform.

**VII.** In 1910, Churchill became the second youngest Home Secretary in British history.

  **A.** As Home Secretary or His Majesty's Principal Secretary of State, Churchill held a post of enormous responsibility.

    **1.** The Home Secretary was effectively responsible for all matters directly involving people living in Great Britain, including law enforcement, labor issues, immigration, censorship, and numerous other issues.

    **2.** Churchill handled all these posts with great ability. He was energetic and innovative, a skilled administrator, and a forceful proponent of good policies. He also took responsibility for his actions.

  **B.** His actions also caused criticism that stayed with him for years.

    **1.** He was criticized for the police action taken against a gang of anarchists in the East End of London (Sydney Street, 1910).

    **2.** The criticism was not so much that he had allowed the anarchists' refuge to burn to the ground when it caught on fire, but rather that it was unseemly for a cabinet member to be present at the scene of the event.

    **3.** He was criticized for his actions in putting down riots by Welsh miners (Tonypandy, 1910). It was said that he had used troops to shoot down miners. In fact, he never sent the troops in; the riots were put down by the police.

    **4.** But the charges stayed with him for decades.

**VIII.** In 1911, Churchill was named First Lord of the Admiralty, the civilian in charge of the British navy. In those days, when Britain ruled the seas, the admiralty was, next to the Prime Minister, the most important government post in the British Empire.

  **A.** Churchill was superb in the position.

  **B.** From 1911 on, Churchill was convinced that war with Germany was inevitable and that it would be the most destructive war the world had ever seen.

  **C.** The carnage of World War I was indeed enormous.

  **D.** Churchill was convinced there was a better way to fight the war than to accept the slaughter of 20,000 men in one day to gain a few yards.

**E.** For that reason, he proposed a campaign in the Dardanelles.

**F.** Unfortunately, the Dardanelles campaign, as executed, was a disaster.

**G.** Churchill received the blame and was forced to resign.

## Essential Reading:

Charmley, *Churchill*, pp. 26–136.

Manchester, *Churchill*, volume I, pp. 339–563.

## Supplementary Reading:

Churchill, *The World Crisis: 1911–1914*.

## Questions to Consider:

1. Do you see similarities between the Tory democracy of Randolph Churchill and Theodore Roosevelt's ideals of progressive Republicanism?

2. Winston Churchill has been called, with some justice, the "architect of the British welfare state." Would you consider this comment a compliment?

# Lecture Four—Transcript
## Political Beginnings

In our last lecture we looked at the life of Winston Churchill between the age of 20 and 25, and we witnessed a remarkable transformation in him. This was the boy who barely got into Sandhurst, who was regarded by his father as a wastrel, and was the despair of his mother whenever she thought about him. Now, in five years we saw him become a war hero, we saw him become a best-selling author, we saw him become a millionaire by today's standards. The questions are: How? Why? Well, in the first place there was ambition, his father didn't recognize the ambition in him certainly, his schoolteachers did not, but it was there—an ambition to achieve. It was an ambition fostered by the neglect of his parents, by his desire to prove himself to his father, and then later on to vindicate his father's memory, because Churchill was devoted to the memory of his father; it made him seek a place in politics. And in his letters to his mother he is clear that he hopes that out of his military career will come medals and will come recognition and that he can use this to build a career in Parliament.

He also educated himself. Out in India he began to read, his mother sent him book upon book, Macaulay, the magnificent essays, and Edward Gibbon, *The Decline and Fall of the Roman Empire*. These were the books he read over and over again to get their magnificent English prose built into his very bones. But he also got the Parliamentary records and he studied the Parliamentary debates for the last twenty years. He also memorized whole sections of his father's speeches. His education in India made him into the master of prose that he then revealed in his books, not just *The Malakand Field Force* (where he's still rather rough), but by the time he is writing about his adventures in South Africa, he is a master of the English prose. His sentences have a rhetorical flourish to them. In 1897, already he had written a little essay for himself on rhetoric. It is the scaffolding of a political career.

But you know, what he thought to be the essence of a truly great speaker is to believe what you are saying; the audience will never go along no matter how beautiful the words are if you are not convinced yourself. He wrote his own speeches, he did not have speechwriters. He at first tried to give them from memory, but later on he would always use notes. But he used the notes in such a manner that it was

©2001 The Teaching Company.

generally assumed that his speeches were extemporaneous. Each of those speeches he said, off the cuff, took 8 to 10 hours to prepare. So meticulous in his preparation, determination, and never giving up—that is the key to his genius. How easy it would have been for him to give up, simply accept the criticism of his father, and become a wastrel. The army was an easy life, you got up about 6:00, you rode horses a bit, you saw to it that your horse was taken care of. From 11:00 to 5:00 you were free, it was too hot in India to do any thing else. Then 5:00 to 8:00 you played polo and then a splendid meal—that is not a bad life, is it? But no, he sought out danger, responsibility. In 1899, before he had gone out to South Africa, he tried to stand for Parliament (Oldham was the constituency) and he lost. That is an easy way to give up: you tried in Parliament, you lost, and after all, had politics been kind to your father? It destroyed him. But, no, he was determined to run again. In fact, when he was in South Africa, when he had been taken in by John Howard there, while he was escaping, one of the men who was helping him was from Oldham. He shook his hand and said, they will all vote for you next time, sir. And Churchill took him up on that and ran again, and it was from the constituency of Oldham that he was elected to Parliament in 1900.

In 1900, Queen Victoria was coming to the end of her long, long reign, having been queen since 1837. The British Empire was the greatest power in the world; it ruled the waves. England was the supreme economic power. Yet, it was also a land with problems, none more so than the tremendous gulf between rich and poor. England was, in those days, a class society that we cannot grasp. The tremendous distinction not just between wealth and but also birth. You could never learn all the morays of the English upper class. A college that might seem like Magdalene to us was pronounced by them as maudlin at Oxford. And everything set you aside: class, wealth and the grinding poverty of those who lived in the cities of England, malnourished, bad teeth, no chance for an education, except perhaps a year or two at a ragged school, as the upper class called it. Really, a vision without much, down into the mines perhaps at twelve or thirteen. And Churchill would say early on: What good is it if we rule the waves, if we cannot flush our own sewers?

He had a sense for the poor. Mrs. Everest, his nurse, ("Woom"), had been his closest figure as he grew up. He had spent many summers and vacations with her, visiting her brother who was in charge of a prison and learning something about the ordinary Englishman's life. Also, about the narrow margin that separated a man like Mrs. Everest's brother, separated his life of some comfort from another of poverty—just lose that job and you were finished. There was at the same time, in Britain, a terrible problem that goes on with Ireland. Ulster will fight, and Ulster will be right—those were the words of Lord Randolph challenging the idea of home rule for Ireland, that this whole island must be kept in the grip of the British. It was a struggle so fierce that in 1914 it would almost bring Britain to civil war; and it was a great force in British politics in 1900. So, it was a land powerful and yet troubled, labor unrest, and on the horizon, the rising might of Germany threatened Britain's command over the sea. The largest army in Europe was building a fleet.

The British Parliament in 1911 was still defined as consisting of three parts: the Crown (the queen); the House of Lords is the second part; and the House of Commons. The queen ruled in Parliament it was said, and in Parliamentary debates, the Mace, the symbol of royal authority, was placed on the table as a sign that the Crown was present. When monetary bills were discussed, it was under the table as a sign of the absolute control of Commons over the purse. The House of Lords could still veto legislation passed by the House of Commons. Britain was, and is, a Parliamentary democracy. It is critical to understand that you do not vote directly for the Prime Minister, the British equivalent of our president. You elect representatives to Parliament and the party that has the largest number of members in Parliament after the election, it chooses the Prime Minister, the leader of its party. Each member of Parliament represents a geographical district (as Churchill represented Oldham for a while, and then later Manchester, and then Dundee). But you do not have to live in that district; this enables, some think, the finest politicians, those most capable, to serve the country without regard to geographical representation.

In 1900, there were two great parties: the Conservatives and the Liberals. It is not easy to see the difference between them. They were drawn from the same aristocracy. Their social relations were very easy one with the other. But, essentially, the Conservative Party represented a tradition that went back to the time when the monarch had some authority. They were more traditional in their values, strongly in support of the Church of England. The Liberals believed that government should play a larger role in granting benefits to the

©2001 The Teaching Company.

poor, a more powerful role for government in carrying out social programs, that taxes should be used in a small degree to redistribute the wealth. Churchill was elected as a Conservative member of Parliament—that is what his father had been. He believed deeply in his father's values of a Tory democracy; that is to say the Conservatives should draw upon the expanding franchise of Britain, with a large number of British who were able to vote (the middle class), and develop a program that would ultimately draw the poor to them as this franchise ever widened. Education for the poor, unemployment benefits, health insurance, recognizing trade unions—these were the principles of his father.

Churchill also had a deep distrust of the Conservative leadership, for they had been the ones who had destroyed his father's political career as he saw it. No sooner had he entered Parliament than he began to work on a biography of his father, ultimately published in 1906. It was an effort to vindicate the memory of his father, the principles for which his father fought. For him, his father, Lord Randolph, represented an England larger than parties, an England that united itself in what was good, and an England that would live on long after the legacy of petty men of politics had passed away. His father's memory was not an asset to Churchill in these early years. His first speech in Parliament was a controversial speech. He praised the Boers for fighting in the field with such bravery. He was accused, like his father, of trying to run imperialism on the cheap. In other words, when he argued against large amounts of money being voted to the army, he was like his father, who wanted an empire but didn't pay for it in terms of a large military. His speech was a prophetic speech. When he talked about army reform, he said, we could never have an army large enough to defeat the Germans. And he warned that all those who believed that the next war would be short, like the War of 1870 between France and Germany, were wrong. The next war will be a war between democracies, he said, it will be a war fought to the bitter end, and it will cost of millions in lives and billions in money.

In 1904, he decided the leave the Conservative Party. The Conservative Party was pushing a policy of tariffs and Churchill, throughout his life, was a great believer in free trade. It is because of free trade, he said, that the goods of the world come to Britain. Tariffs will raise the food prices for the poor. So, he broke with the Conservative Party, he crossed the aisles, as it was called, and became a member of the Liberal Party. He did it on the basis of principal. But his opponents, the Conservative Party, said he was just an opportunist. He never really gained the full support of many in the Liberal Party, thinking that he had also done it out of political opportunism, that he would get promoted much more quickly if he were in the Liberal Party.

In fact, by 1905, he would become the Undersecretary for the Colonies, his first real post in the government. The Prime Minister forms a government, fills the Chancellor, the Exchequer, the Foreign Secretary, numerous posts, and to hold one of these posts you must be a member of Parliament—it is very different than our system. It blends the legislative and the executive branch. Churchill, as a member of Parliament became Undersecretary for the Colonies. Immediately he was assigned an extremely difficult task—he did not have that adroit sense that a true careerist has, not to take a hard task, take a simple task, take a task that isn't going to make you enemies—he took a very controversial tasks, the final settlement with South Africa with the Boers. The constitution that was developed under his auspices was a prime example of his view that once you have conquered, you must be magnanimous. Greatness of spirit, that is the mark of a great man, and Churchill always had it. To hold out the hand to those you have conquered, and his speech says we do not have "one man one vote" in our country, but is not a reason we should not have it in South Africa. It can be a model to us. Let the ordinary Boer—farmer, worker, artisan—let him vote and let him keep his language. I have no problem whatsoever, he said, with Dutch teachers teaching the Dutch language to Dutch children. Our English tongue does not need to be forced artificially upon anyone. Let them have that pride, let them have that ethnic identity. South Africa would never be a land without problems, but the constitution he established would guide South Africa through the Second World War and tie it deeply to the British Empire.

He then received his first Cabinet level post in 1908 when he became President of the Board of Trade. This is all a very rapid rise, don't you see. President of the Board of Trade is like being Secretary of Commerce. Churchill plunged himself into a program of social reform. He associated himself with figures like Beatrice and Sydney Webb, reading deeply the literature about the poverty of England and working to establish a program of welfare benefits. His son would call Winston Churchill "the architect of the welfare state." It has always made it difficult for strong right wing Conservatives to appreciate Churchill. He was never a party man—he was never a Conservative, he was never a Liberal. He believed in freedom, and he believed that the ordinary man and woman should have a safety net beneath them to catch them if they fell and to serve as a springboard to come back up to the top. The difference between liberalism and socialism, he said, is that socialism wants to tear down the rich, liberalism wants to raise up the poor.

In 1910, he became Home Secretary. It is not unusual at all in British politics to move rapidly from one position to the other, and Home Secretary is a position of enormous responsibility. The Home Secretary is essentially responsible for all aspects of the relationship of the British subject inside Britain itself. Home Secretary is in charge of prisons, censorship, labor—all of these matters fell to Churchill. It was a daunting task, and he set about it with characteristic energy, characteristic study, and characteristic administrative ability. When his enemies said that he was impetuous, they gave no attention whatsoever to the enormous care and success in which he managed his bureaus on a day-to-day basis, as he did as Home Secretary. He made enemies, and he took actions that would stay with him for the rest of his life. We talk about the long ago events, events that in our own world would be forgotten in a week or two because of the nature of the media, these were events that would be brought up against Churchill years later. For example, there were anarchists all over Europe in those days. They did like things like assassinate major Russian leaders. There were anarchists in Britain, particularly in London and the area around Whitechapel, a place where Joseph Stalin lived for a few months when he was on the lam from the Russian police. And the anarchists killed policemen.

Churchill, as Home Secretary, went down to a scene where anarchists had taken up refuge in a house on Sydney Street. They killed four policemen. Troops were brought out because the police did not have satisfactory weapons to go up against the well-armed urban terrorists (as we would call them today), and they were shooting it out with the police. The house caught on fire, and Churchill forbid the fire department to put it out since the anarchists were still firing at them. The anarchists were burned to death, and Churchill was criticized not so much for that, but that it was unseemly for a member of the Cabinet to be there on the scene. Churchill should have stayed away from it. Well, that is not the way to deal with a matter like that, he needed to be right there managing it, to keep it from getting out of control. But years later, cartoons and political enemies would bring up Sydney Street as an example of his impetuosity, that zig-zag crazy motion in his brain. One of his best friends would say, talking about Sydney Street later on, "Winston is like a chauffer who drives you week after week with perfect safety, and then suddenly, one day drives over a cliff and kills you."

So he had Sydney Street, and then, minors in Wales went on strike. They were crushed by the grinding poverty and the intention of their bosses to drop their wages even further to wring out a bit more profit. Now, Churchill sent in the police and he ordered up troops, but he never sent the troops in. The minors who rioted were put down by police, not by troops. But years later, Tonypandy (as it was called) was brought up, and it was said, as an article of faith by the Labor Party, Churchill shot down minors. That is not true. Now, that same year there was a great railroad strike and food could not get through to the people of Liverpool and Manchester and other cities. Then he did use troops to bring the strikers back in line and to let the food go again. But don't you see the difference? No troops against minors who were striking for their rights, but troops used to make sure people didn't starve—it is setting priorities and it is taking the responsibility, because he always took responsibility. How easy, he said, it would be for me to simply put somebody between myself and these problems, and let them take the blows. But I will never take that cowardly route, let the blows come hard again and again where I do what is right.

In 1911, he became First Lord of the Admiralty. In those days, when Britain ruled the waves, the civilian in charge of the British fleet was arguably, next to the Prime Minister, the most important single figure in the British government. Churchill loved the Admiralty; he loved the fleet. He was innovative, not only did he begin to establish a naval flying core, he learned to fly himself (to the terror of his wife, for he was now married), crashing from time to time, going up, scaring his instructors half to death with his daring flying habits, but learning how flying worked. Also, he recognized the ever-growing menace of Germany. From 1911 on, he was convinced that war would come with Germany and that it would be the most terrifying war, the most destructive war the world had ever seen. So, on June 28, in a Europe that looked upon itself as being at the pinnacle of prosperity, in a Europe where many thought no war would ever come

 ©2001 The Teaching Company.

again (at least that no European armies would ever fight each other again), in the town of Sarajevo, the heir to the Austro-Hungarian empire was shot down by a terrorist. The Austrians demanded satisfaction. They sent a note to the Serbs demanding that these terrorists be rooted out and that the Austrians be allowed to supervise the destruction of this terrorism, supervising the Serbians. The Serbs agreed to every demand, except they asked for international mediation on the question of the Austrians coming in and supervising their police. But Austria wanted war; it wanted to root out Serbs and terrorism forever.

So, on July 28, war was declared by Austria upon Serbia. Europe was divided into a number of alliances: France, Russia, and Britain owing a general moral commitment to France, Austria, and Germany. So, the great machine went into motion. At the last moment, Kaiser Wilhelm and the Czar of Russia, his cousin, Nikki, wanted to hold it back, but the general said there was no way to stop the mobilization. Once the mobilization was underway the German High Command demanded the right to march through Belgium, a neutral country bound to Britain by a treaty. They offered to pay the Belgians compensation. The king of the Belgium said, we are a nation not a road. And so Germany invaded. The war came, and Britain, for a scrap of paper (which is what the Germans called the treaty that the British had with Belgium), went to war and the guns of August fired. By the time that month was over—one month—206,000 French soldiers had been killed or wounded. By the time that year was over, 95,000 British troops lay dead and no country could afford to make peace; they would topple from power.

The slaughter began on the western front. Churchill, as first Lord of the Admiralty, felt deeply that there was another way to fight this war than simply sending brave men over no-man's-land into machine guns, accepting 20,000 dead in one day to gain a few yards. So, with the full assent of the Cabinet, with the chiefs of staff in agreement, he put forth a bold plan to change the course of the war. In January 1915, the Dardanelles campaign began to develop. British and French ships would force the Hellespont (that place where Europe and Asia come together, where mighty Xerzes had crossed so many centuries before), to force the Dardanelles, as we call it now, and to capture Constantinople. Turkey was already a member of the alliance with Germany and Austria; this would knock the Turks out of the war and give Russia a victory that would enable them to stay, because Russian troops could then occupy Constantinople and have a glorious victory for an army that was much pressed. The admiral on the spot, Sackville Carden, the British admiral said, we can take the Straits, we can force them. So it began, on February 19, the British and French fleet attacked the Turkish forts all along the Straits. In one day of bombardment they all but collapsed and then caution set in. A month would pass. The admiral—harassed by Churchill, who kept saying, you have knocked out the forts, now take the rest of the Straits—resigned, his second in command took it up.

In one day, March 18, they blasted the rests of the forts out of the way and the passage to Constantinople lay open. And when some of his ships were sunk by mines, he hesitated. Then the mediocre minds inside the war cabinet began to get worried. Troops were landed in April, and by May it had become one more stalemate. The Turkish troops, strengthened by German officers, fed with large amounts of ammunition and heavy guns, held the British and French troops. The brave troops from Australia and New Zealand there on the beaches. "Everywhere there was slaughter, bloody bodies and bloody bandages, the whole of the water turned red," Churchill's brother, who was serving there, wrote back.

Although it had been approved by the whole Cabinet, though it had been approved by the chiefs of staff, Churchill took the blame. A man of cast iron principles, everything stuck to him. The politicians began to tremble. The Prime Minister, Herbert Asquith, was determined to form a new government that would bring the Conservative Party in a national government to fight this war, and the Conservative Party had one demand, we want Churchill's scalp. So, Asquith brought Churchill in and said I am forming a new government, what we can do for you? I want to stay on as the Admiralty. Sorry, that is no longer possible. So, the Dardanelles became one more and, indeed, the greatest stain upon Churchill in the mind of the British public, stripped of the Admiralty, put into a humiliating minor office, he went to his constituents in Dundee, he did not make an attack upon the government, he said, all that is passed, I did my best. What we must do as a people is unite the ordinary worker working for the war effort, the women and children at home, the soldiers in the field. For beyond all this carnage, I see the liberty of Britain illuminated by the freedom and grandeur of a peaceful Europe—that must be our goal.

                      ©2001 The Teaching Company.

# Lecture Five
# Churchill and Controversy

**Scope:**

Churchill was—and for some historians still is—a controversial figure. Many of his personal qualities tended to provoke controversy, including his refusal to "stay in his box," to compromise his vision, and to avoid difficult decisions. The Dardanelles campaign was a major controversy and seminal event in Churchill's life. It turned into a disaster because of Churchill's impetuosity and his inability to interpret human character and recognize those who bore him ill. The tragic failure of that campaign, and the public and political response to it, threatened to destroy Churchill's political career. His own response embodied those personal qualities that enabled him not only to survive but, ultimately, to triumph.

## Outline

I.   Why was Churchill plagued with controversy all his life?

    **A.** Churchill was a genius and genius is often distrusted and envied, especially in the political world.

    **B.** Churchill did not "stay in his box"; he always went above and beyond his responsibilities.

        **1.** As First Lord of the Admiralty, he went beyond what was considered his sphere of responsibility—solely to manage the budget. He worked hard to transform the navy (to get bigger guns, build faster warships, and switch the basic fuel from coal to oil).

        **2.** He did not take advice from his admirals. Instead, he took advice from what many in the admiralty considered to be bad sources, such as Sir John Fisher, who was considered somewhat quirky.

        **3.** He wanted to develop the military potential of aircraft, against the opinion of many in the military who saw aircraft as merely sports vehicles.

        **4.** In 1914, in an effort to defend Antwerp from the Germans, Churchill shipped Royal Marines and naval reserves to the Belgian port and went into battle with them. This was not his decision to make as First Lord of the Admiralty. Eventually, Antwerp collapsed as the Germans prevailed, and the troops had to be recalled.

   5. This action became the subject of ridicule in the press, and Churchill was severely reprimanded for his over-enthusiasm.

   6. Later, the King of the Belgians declared that he thought no action did more to secure victory in World War I than that of Antwerp. By holding on in Antwerp, Churchill's action enabled the British to send more troops to Calais and other ports, with the result that they were never captured.

   7. But the idea that Antwerp was a fiasco stuck to Churchill's character, and official reports would never remove the blame that tainted him.

**C.** Other factors that made Churchill "untrustworthy" in the eyes of his peers included the legacy of his father, Lord Randolph.

   1. Churchill did not distance himself from his father, a man with a bad reputation.

   2. Instead, he wrote a defensive biography of Lord Randolph, which was greatly criticized.

**D.** Churchill had an incisive tongue.

**E.** He did not have "antennae" when it came to judging character, he did not recognize those who threatened his career, and he often mistook an enemy for a friend.

   1. One such figure was Horatio Kitchener, who had never liked Churchill, although he was outwardly friendly to him.

   2. Kitchener, and others in the Cabinet, set Churchill up for failure in the Dardanelles campaign.

**II.** The Dardanelles was a seminal event in Churchill's life. Churchill's wife spoke of his "grief" over the Dardanelles; she thought he would never get over this particular disaster.

**A.** Churchill's boldest policy to break the stalemate on the western front was to advocate a campaign against the Dardanelles, that strip of land that separates Asia from Europe, near Istanbul (Constantinople).

**B.** Churchill wanted to send British troops into the Dardanelles, knock out the Turkish forts (Turkey was an ally of Germany and Austria), capture Constantinople, sweep up through the Balkans, capture Vienna, and then move on to Germany.

**C.** But Kitchener, and most of the British High Command, thought that the war could be won only by killing Germans in France.

**D.** They agreed, however, to let Churchill go ahead with his plan.

    **1.** The plan was implemented too quickly.

    **2.** Foreign allies could not agree on their roles; the Greeks did not want to share the capture of Constantinople with the Russians.

    **3.** Then the Greek government fell to a pro-German regime.

    **4.** The British admiral was aging, and his strategy was inefficient; he resigned, and a new admiral replaced him in the middle of the attack on Constantinople.

    **5.** Several of the British ships were sunk.

    **6.** Sir Ian Hamilton, an old friend of Churchill, went out to the Mediterranean (with an out-of-date map of Gallipoli and an out-of-date handbook on the Turkish army). He recommended that a large number of troops be sent in.

    **7.** Kitchener wanted all his troops for fighting on the western front.

    **8.** By the time troops were landed, the Turks were well entrenched, and led by the Germans.

**E.** Churchill, led on by his own impetuosity and his weak "antennae," had rushed into the disaster. Furthermore, he did not understand how weak his position was.

**F.** The press, fed by leaks from his fellow ministers, hounded Churchill.

**G.** By the time the British troops withdrew in January 1916, Britain had suffered 213,980 casualties to achieve nothing.

**H.** Churchill received the blame, accepted the responsibility, and resigned from his post as First Lord of the Admiralty.

**III.** Churchill had few real friends who would stick with him to the end.

**A.** Even the Liberal leader David Lloyd George, whom Churchill had considered a good friend, offered Churchill no support after the Dardanelles disaster.

**B.** The Prime Minister, Lord Asquith, refused to allow Churchill to speak in his own defense, which was customary in such circumstances.

**IV.** Churchill could have told all about the horrors of World War I, but he did not. Instead, he asked for a field command and was sent out for training in the Grenadier Guards.

   **A.** He was not, at first, well received, but he trained without complaint and was rewarded with the position of lieutenant colonel in the Royal Scots Fusiliers.

   **B.** He served beside his men on the western front in the spring of 1916.

   **C.** His men told him that there was no better loved commander on the entire western front than Churchill.

## Essential Reading:
Churchill, *World Crisis: 1915*.

## Supplementary Reading:
James, *Churchill*, pp. 3–106; *Gallipoli*.
Moorehead, *Gallipoli*.

## Questions to Consider:
1. Do you believe that Churchill's strategy for the Dardanelles campaign was flawed from the start?
2. Unlike Ronald Reagan, Churchill was not Teflon. Why?

©2001 The Teaching Company.

# Lecture Five—Transcript
# Churchill and Controversy

In our last lecture, we explored the first part of Churchill's political life. We saw him enter Parliament at the age of 26, in 1900, when Queen Victoria was still alive. And we saw him rise very rapidly, in part due to his change of parties, switching from the Conservative Party to the Liberal Party in 1904, then, moving rapidly through a series of government posts (remembering always that in the British system to be in the Cabinet you must also be a member of Parliament). So he is both a member of Parliament as well as serving in the Liberal Party government. We saw him as Undersecretary for the Colonies, played an important role in the settlement of South Africa as president of the Board of Trade (essentially as Secretary of Commerce), then as Home Secretary, and then at the very early age 37 becoming First Lord of Admiralty, the civilian in charge of the British navy. At that period, when the British navy was all crucial and powerful, to be First Lord of Admiralty was perhaps second only to the Prime Minister in importance. That importance grew with the coming of the Great War in 1914. We took Churchill through the disastrous campaign at the Dardanelles in 1915, which would force him to resign from the government on May 15, 1915.

The Dardanelles was a seminal event in Churchill's political life, indeed, in his life as a whole. He would never fully get over the disaster that was the Dardanelles. Years later, with all the success behind him, after leading Britain to victory in the Second World War, he would write that he had ruined himself for a period as a result of trying to undertake a great enterprise from a position of subordinate authority. His wife, Clementine, said, I thought Winston would die of grief over the Dardanelles. I thought he would never get over it.

It has been used as a test case by historians who do not share my admiration for Churchill. A book, for example, *Churchill: 1900-1939, A Study in Failure*, looks upon the Dardanelles as typical of why Churchill was ultimately a failure. I think we, too, should look at the Dardanelles, explore it in some depth. We start from the point of view of Churchill as a minister; we ask the question why he inspired such distrust among very important colleagues. One of his colleagues in the Admiralty said Churchill is a greater danger than the Germans by far. Another said, I would much rather Winston on the other side than with us. Why? Why this dislike that would play a crucial role in his fall? He did not "stay in a box." Churchill was a genius, he was a political genius, a genius as a statesman in the same way that Julius Caesar was, and genius invokes distrust. One of Churchill's friends said that: "much of the envy and malice against Churchill came from the distrust with which mediocrity views genius at close quarters."

Very few geniuses get to top in the political world. I have tried several times to think of geniuses in our own political world; I have not come up with one yet. In the corporate world, no doubt. In the world of law and medicine, geniuses always rise to the top. Certainly not in the academic world, the only two geniuses I know of who were teachers were Socrates and Jesus and both came to a very bad end. Socrates said it is envy that has brought me here. And Pilate recognized that it was out of envy that Jesus was delivered up to him. An old professor of mine said that in the academic world, "A" people will sometimes vote for "A" people; "C" people will sometimes vote for "A" people; but "B" people (mediocrities) always vote for "C" people.

So it is in the world of politics, which Winston Churchill lived. After all, he is suspicious, he writes books, lots of books, and they sell very, very well. He is a powerful, spellbinding speaker in Parliament. Those are worrisome things on their own. But he doesn't "stay in his box." As First Lord of the Admiralty, in the view of his colleagues and in the view of the navy (the Royal Sailors), his job was to fight to get them the largest budget possible, but Churchill did not see it that way. In 1911, he was working to transform the navy. He worked to get bigger guns—replacing 13-and-a-half inch guns with 15 inch guns—all good and true, but he shouldn't be doing that. Let us the sailors being doing that, don't you see? It is not for him to tell us, we still want 13-and-a-half inch guns. Let's have them. Then, building fast warships, and along with that, to make these faster warships work, switching over from coal to oil. These were all very important innovations. He saw to it that they happened. But the sailors didn't like it (the admirals didn't like it, that is who I mean by the sailors). Then, he took advice from bad sources in their view. Come to me, I am the Acting Admiralty-in-charge. I am First Sea Lord. No, he relied upon a retired admiral, John Fisher. Sir John Fisher had a reputation for being kind of strange himself, and in retirement he had grown even stranger. But he was Winston Churchill's main source of

©2001 The Teaching Company.

advice on these changes. People would say with considerable justification: Winston is not a good picker, he doesn't choose good people to support him, he is quirky in how he chooses.

Then the war breaks out. Churchill is very interested in flying, and he develops a Royal Naval Flying Core as well. That again is something "out of the box." The admirals, like the generals, were convinced that aircraft was only for sport; it would never play a role in warfare. Then there was that tragic business at Antwerp, that foolish business at Antwerp. By October 1914, the Germans had been unable to break through and capture Paris, but their mighty war machine was still on the march. They were determined to capture all of the ports that dominate the English Channel, right down to Calais, because if they had those ports, the British would have enormous difficulty in shipping troops and supplies to France. They were moving upon Antwerp, and the Belgian army was barely holding on. They were shattered by the ceaseless German bombardments, the German capture of their forts that were regarded as invincible. And Churchill decided that Antwerp must be held. But that was not his decision as First Lord of Admiralty—that was for the army—but not only did he decided it must be held, he shipped troops, he shipped Royal Marines (over which he certainly had technical command) and then two units of recently recruited Naval Reserves as they were called. One of these Naval Reserves that went over was Rupert Brook, a great poet who would die in the Dardanelles campaign. The other was the son of the Prime Minister. They went over to Antwerp, and Churchill went with them. And for seven days he led the defense of Antwerp, rushing around. Someone described him like "a hero in a melodrama, rushing up on his horse to save the day." He moved in the trenches, he held the Belgian's on, until, finally, after seven days, they did collapse and the troops had to be withdrawn.

This, in the newspaper, became the subject of ridicule. Why is the First Lord of Admiralty over there fighting the battle, and why did we send those troops over there at all? They had to be withdrawn—it was a fiasco. Such was also the view in the Cabinet itself. Churchill was severely reprimanded for this over-enthusiasm. Later on, the King of the Belgians, in 1918, said that he thought no action more secured victory than Antwerp. He could never understand why the British made it a subject of ridicule. By holding on, it enabled there to be enough British troops at Calais and other ports so that they were never captured. But the idea that it was a fiasco stuck to

Churchill, and this is another aspect of Churchill's character. It is difficult to explain, but things stuck to him—blame and years of explanation, official reports would never remove these claims that clung to him. Antwerp would remain in the mind of the press, and the public, and most of his fellow Cabinet members as a fiasco.

There were other qualities that Churchill had that made him, in the eyes of his fellow Cabinet members, not trustworthy. First, there was the legacy of his father; Churchill gloried in the legacy of Lord Randolph. An astute young politician would have distanced himself from his father, not Churchill. He wrote a biography of his father in which he heaped abuse upon those who'd abused his father. Now, his father had the reputation of being untrustworthy, of being a political adventurer, of always scheming, and this, too, rubbed off on Winston. Then, yes, he was a powerful speaker. He could also be very sarcastic. The right, honorable gentleman is one of those speakers, who, before he gets up, does not know what he is going to say, while he speaking, does not know what he is saying, and when he is finished, does not know what he has said—it just does not win you friends.

Now, Churchill thought it was wonderful that Parliament had this tradition of give and take. Well, maybe it did, but it also had people with very long memories. Churchill also did not have antennae. In our first lecture, I said he had a moral compass. A political career depends upon antennae. Churchill could never read people, what they were really thinking about him. So, because he went to their dinner parties, he stayed at their country homes, he thought these people were his friends—they weren't and he was a threat. He didn't understand politics. Politics is a very bloody business—to stay on top you must recognize who is the greatest threat to your job and figure a way to get rid of them.

The war, too, was different than anyone had ever seen. Wars are places where generals and admirals win reputation—that is what they live for. Yet this was a war like none that had ever been before: carnage on a vast scale, enormous fronts, and no way to bring it to an end. And guiding Britain's strategy during this period was the great figure of Horatio Kitchener—Lord Kitchener, Kitchener of Khartoum—with his great swirling mustaches, huge beefy figure, he looked down at you from recruiting posters all over Britain, all over the empire: I want you. He was building a new army. He was so powerful and so much a myth in the public mind that he could not be contradicted—whatever he said, went. Lord Kitchener had a long memory. He had never liked Churchill. He had not liked Churchill being sent out to him during the expedition that ended in the Battle of Omdurman. As Churchill said, "it was a case of dislike before first sight," and he had never liked Churchill after that. He was friendly with him, seemed sympathetic, but he, like others in the Cabinet, were setting Churchill up for failure. If the lives of 213,000 men depended upon this, so be it, such is the cost of war.

So the Dardanelles campaign was indeed the brainchild of Churchill. It was the desire to break with the slaughter on the western front and to carry out this bold sweeping movement as we saw in our last lecture. Do you remember, we were going to force the Dardanelles, knock off the Turkish forts, capture Constantinople, and then turn in a great sweeping flank action, move up through the Balkans, capture Vienna, knocking Austria out of the war, then turn upon Germany. Well, Kitchener and most of the High Command did not like this idea to start with. They knew how the war would be won: it would be won by killing Germans in France. It was just that simple. They did not want someone like Churchill telling them otherwise. Their careers and reputations were based upon this, but if he were determined to do it, go ahead.

The Cabinet agrees, Kitchener agrees, the admiral on the spot agrees, but the strategy was always flawed. First of all, it was put together too rapidly. On January 5, they got a telegram from Admiral Carden saying—it is possible by February, they were going into action. Now, how do you take Constantinople without troops? The idea was it could be done with just ships. But how? Someone has to occupy it. Well, the Russians will send troops. Well, they had not gotten this clear with the Czar. Once he heard about it, he thought it was a good idea. He was going to take Constantinople, but the Greeks also wanted Constantinople. And Churchill said, well, they can send us 60,000 troops. Yes, but we don't want the Czar in Constantinople; we want us, the Greeks, in Constantinople. So, neither side ever sent troops and the Greek government fell and a pro-German government took over before any of this could get started.

Then, the admiral on the spot wasn't the man to do this—Churchill should have understood this—he was an old man; he had never really had military experience in battles at sea, he had been charge of the fleet at Malta, the dockyards at Malta. He didn't follow up his opportunity. He fired in February and forts were stilled, but nothing was then done until March. He resigned and the new admiral had to be put in his place, John Robeck, but right there, changing in mid-stream, that is worrisome, and Churchill should have gotten worried. Instead, the fleet goes out on February 18, it knocked out all the forts, and then one of the ships, a French ship, the *Bouvet* is sunk by a mine and then three more, the *Irresistible*, the *Inflexible*, the *Ocean* are sunk. Suddenly the navy is in a panic. So they say, we need troops.

By this time you ought to be re-examining the situation, but no, goaded by Churchill, the Cabinet goes ahead and says, let's send an army man out. The choice could not be more suited to Churchill than his old friend, Sir Ian Hamilton; he even wrote a book about Sir Ian Hamilton's glorious march in South Africa. Sir Ian Hamilton had recommended Churchill for the Victoria Cross, Britain's highest medal for valor for Churchill's actions for the war in South Africa. Ian Hamilton goes out without even really landing on the beaches, with an out-of-date map of Gallipoli and with an out-of-date handbook on the Turkish army. He stays on the island of Lemnos, sails around a bit, and says, you have to have troops to do this. Well, what is an army man going to say except "you have to have troops to do this, and we need lots of troops"? It is this at this very moment that Lord Kitchener refuses to send the troops that he has promised; they are needed on the western front he insists. So, weeks drag on, and then, when the troops are landed, the Turks are well entrenched, well led by the Germans.

Do you see it is a set up for failure? But Churchill's impetuosity, his lack of antennae lead him to rush on into this, until it becomes a disaster. Then he does not understand how weak his position is; he does not understand the swirl of hostility around him. The press is baying at him—where are they getting so much of their information about Churchill's folly? From his fellow ministers who are leaking this information. The fiasco is so terrible that by the time the British finally withdraw, there are 213,000 casualties for no gain whatsoever. It is the single most humiliating defeat in the entire First World War for the British, and a fall guy has to be found. You cannot say the whole Cabinet wanted this, then the whole Cabinet should step down. There has to be one person to fix the blame upon and it is Churchill. The liberal government that has been conducting

 ©2001 The Teaching Company.

the war up until this time under Herbert Asquith can only stay in power if the Conservative Party is willing to form a coalition with it. The Conservatives had their long memories and they demand that Churchill be removed, and it is done in the most brutal fashion, he is simply gone from the admiralty. Then to add to the humiliation, he is given the most insignificant post in the Cabinet, the Duchy of Lancaster who has no responsibilities accept to appoint justices of the peace. For politics is not only about ruining someone, it is about humiliating them, as well.

Now, Churchill's qualities played a large role in this happening to him. The very thing that made him a great statesman—his moral compass—set him up with his lack of antennae for this terrible fall; his refusal to stay in a box. His inability to make real friends, Churchill had people who were devoted to him, who admired him enormously, he also had a lot of people in high position who hated him, but he had few real friends who would stick with him to the end. In fact, the man who played the greatest role in overthrowing him was David Lloyd George. He and Churchill had been—Churchill thought—close friends, and certainly colleagues in forcing through much of the welcome legislation of 1908, 1909, and 1910. But they were very different: LLoyd George came from a Welch mining family; he had been raised by a widowed mother; he was a totally self-made man. He and Churchill, Churchill thought, were friends. Well, as Mrs. Churchill tried to convince her husband at the time of the Dardanelles—David is the one who turned you in, David is the one who ruined you, David is your Judas—Churchill could never believe it. He went to Lloyd George and said you have to go intercede; you really control how this new government is going to be set up, regardless of what Herbert wants to do; you control it. David said, you will have to go. And Churchill said, you don't care if I am ruined, you don't care if my enemies trample me under foot. Then, wrapping himself in patriotism, Lloyd George said, I don't care for myself either at this moment, all I want to do is win the war.

Then there was this lunatic Admiral Fisher, John Fisher, remember? Churchill's source of advice on redoing the navy. Churchill had brought him back into the Admiralty. He had been the one to push Churchill to go for the Dardanelles. Then, at the critical moment, he resigned, saying that Churchill is the one who is more dangerous than the Germans. When Churchill said, please stay on at the Admiralty, he wrote a note off to all of Churchill's political enemies saying he has offered me 30 pieces of silver, this Judas, but I will not betray my country. Now that is being a bad picker to think some one like Fisher is in your corner. Again, Mrs. Churchill tried to say, Winston, this man is a lunatic, I had him to lunch, the way you requested, just Jack Fisher and me, we had lunch, it seemed very pleasant, you were off in Paris (and Churchill was in fact off in Paris, he was negotiating to bring Italy into the war at that very moment with the British), you were off in Paris and he left, I thought he was gone, I started down the hall, he jumped out at me and said, you foolish woman, you think Winston is off in Paris but in fact he is with his mistress at this very moment. He is deranged, watch out for him. But Winston sails on, thinking everyone is as true as he is.

Then the debate over the Dardanelles in the late spring and summer of that year, in 1915—Why is the First Lord of Admiralty always away from his office, never there? Well, in fact, he had been away since the start of the war, from August 1914 until May 1915, for fourteen days (seven of them in Antwerp and the rest in Paris negotiating to bring Italy into the war). It was a critical move to bring the Italians into the war. But, I don't know why he is away so much. I don't think he has been away that much. But worst of all, Churchill goes to the Prime Minister and says, I would like you, if you would want to, to see the speech I am going to make. Having laid down my office as First Lord of Admiralty, I am going to make my speech to Parliament (which was standard). The Prime Minister's agreement was necessary but was given as just a formality. The Prime Minister said, I am sorry, old boy, I don't think that would be appropriate at the moment. But, I must be able to defend myself. No, I am afraid things are a bit too delicate at the moment, perhaps later. So, he is denied the right to speak out for himself at that critical moment when it was all still fresh. That is politics.

What does he do then? Well, we know what a politician would do today, he would step back, sign a huge contract, and write a tell all book—what is really going on with the war, learn the truth—isn't that right? Five, six million dollar contract, huge royalties. Well, why not? Have these people been loyal to you? And the war is a mess, Lloyd George himself said the war department keeps three sets of figures: one to fool the public, one to fool the Cabinet, and one to fool themselves. Now, it is a horrible mess, and the Cabinet knows if the public really understood the mindless slaughter that was going on… Today, you can still go into a British village with seven houses

   ©2001 The Teaching Company.

there and see, on the First World War monument, the names of twenty-one boys killed. When, at the Battle of Somme, in 1916, 20,000 British troops are killed in one day and the slaughter went on. In 1917, in Passchendaele, General Haig sent the same kind of brave boys into the machine guns with staggering losses. One of his lieutenant generals went out finely attired in whipcord britches and high boots, swagger stick, got out of his car and suddenly began to weep. He had no idea in his chateau eating croissants that the men were slogging through mud up to their knees trying to reach these machine guns. He wept and said, God forgive us for having sent men to fight in this.

So, Churchill could have told all, but he didn't. No, instead, after staying briefly in this post as the Duchy of Lancaster, he said, I want a command. Will you give me one? Will you give me a command in the field? So, he was sent out to do training. He thought he might get to be a general. But no, they weren't going to let him be a general, but they said if you show yourself to train well, we will give it some more thought. So he was sent to the Grenadier Guards for two months of training starting in November. When he got there he was told, you understand we were not consulted about your coming out here. He was met with stone silence from the officers. You can stay in that dugout they told him—one foot deep in water—and yet he won them over. He was always out for extra practice on the machine gun range, rifle range, took every dirty assignment. Then they gave him his command, lieutenant colonel in the Royal Scots Fusiliers, and he went up to the front. He served beside his men in savage fighting. Quiet sector of the front, on a quiet day a thousand British soldiers died just from shelling, and Churchill was there. He kept his dugout as close to the front as possible. He went out on night patrols, where they would bring back German prisoners. How proud I am of these men, he said, my soldiers, fierce with their clubs and helmets. He always wore a French style helmet—it gave him a little better protection. One night they were out patrolling and he suddenly shouted out, damn you, who's got that light going? They said, sir, it is you, you have snapped your flashlight on by mistake. Oh I am sorry, he said. At the end, soldiers told him, there is no better-loved commander on this entire front than you. He won them over—brave, resolute, true—he served all through the spring of 1916, once again, as he had done on the northwest frontier, at Omdurman, South Africa, showing that resolute bravery and character.

©2001 The Teaching Company.

# Lecture Six
# Post-War Challenges

**Scope:**

In 1917, Churchill was cleared of blame for the Dardanelles disaster, yet the incident would continue to plague his reputation for many years. In David Lloyd George's Liberal government, Churchill held several major and problematic posts. In 1919, he became Minister for War and Air and found himself facing the difficult task of demobilization. In 1921, he became Colonial Secretary, a position that brought with it the unenviable responsibility for handling problems in Ireland and the Middle East. Throughout the 1920s, Churchill warned against the rise of Soviet communism and advocated an offensive strategy to deal with it. For his troubles, he was accused of being a warmonger. In 1925, with the demise of the Liberal Party, Churchill returned to the Conservative Party, which again gained him the reputation of being a political adventurer. Under Prime Minister Stanley Baldwin, Churchill rose to the powerful position of Chancellor of the Exchequer.

# Outline

I. In 1917, an investigative committee cleared Churchill of any blame in the Dardanelles disaster.

  A. Yet the blame for the Dardanelles would continue to haunt Churchill for many years; as the saying goes, slander moves in six-league boots.

  B. The Prime Minister, now David Lloyd George, brought Churchill back into the government as Minister of Munitions.
    1. In this position, Churchill continued to develop the concept of the armored tank, first conceived by him when he was First Lord of the Admiralty.
    2. He also had the foresight to vigorously support the development of air power during the last phase of World War I.

  C. Throughout the rest of World War I and in the 1920s, Churchill continued to hold major government posts.

©2001 The Teaching Company.

1. In 1919, he was named Minister for War and Air. Because another war was unthinkable to the British military establishment, Churchill followed the wishes of the Government and Parliament to cut the military budget.
2. His job would be demobilization; his policy was to bring home the troops based on their length of duty in the war.

**II.** Churchill warned vigorously against communism.

    **A.** After World War I, Churchill wanted to redeploy troops to Russia to fight the Bolsheviks. He believed that socialism and communism rested on the denial of a fundamental human freedom: the right to property.

    **B.** For this view, he was called a warmonger.

    **C.** The British government ultimately did nothing.

    **D.** The British Labour Party and many British workers criticized Churchill for his hostility toward Bolshevism, which they interpreted as a hostility toward labor in general.

**III.** In 1921, Churchill was made Colonial Secretary.

    **A.** The position of Colonial Secretary was a difficult one in 1921.

    **B.** The British Empire reached its height at the end of World War I.

    **C.** Churchill had to deal with problems in Ireland and the Middle East.

    **D.** Churchill went to the Middle East with T. E. Lawrence, who believed Britain had strong commitments to the Arabs, which left no room for a Jewish state.

        1. Churchill was a friend of Zionist leaders.
        2. He believed in the idea of a Jewish state, even if it meant taking land away from the Arabs.
        3. His views gained him enemies in Middle Eastern countries, and he was opposed by major figures in the British government and army.

    **E.** He also had to deal with the question of home rule for Ireland, which had been a violent issue for many years.

        1. When he served as Minister of War, he sent troops to Ireland, the Blacks and Tans, who fought against the IRA terrorists.

2. As Colonial Secretary, Churchill began to negotiate with the IRA.

3. The compromise they established remains today: that northern Ireland (Ulster) would remain part of Britain and a free state would be created in the rest of Ireland, which would eventually become the Republic of Ireland.

IV. The demise of the Liberal Party led Churchill to return to the Conservative Party in 1925.

    **A.** This switch of political parties again made enemies in both parties for Churchill, who was accused of being a "political adventurer."

    **B.** Under Baldwin, the new Prime Minister, Churchill became Chancellor of the Exchequer, considered the most important position leading to the position of Prime Minister.

**Essential Reading:**

Churchill, *The World Crisis: 1918–1928*.

Manchester, *Churchill*, volume I, pp. 563–736.

**Supplementary Reading:**

Charmley, *Churchill*, pp. 139–237.

James, *Churchill*, pp. 109–150.

**Questions to Consider:**

1. What credit and what blame is due Churchill for the continuing situation in Northern Ireland and the Middle East?

2. Would history have been different if Churchill had been able to deploy British troops against the Bolsheviks in Russia in 1919?

# Lecture Six—Transcript
## Post-War Challenges

In our last lecture we explored in depth the Dardanelles crisis, the campaign, and its impact upon Winston Churchill; his fall from political influence; and his response to go into the trenches and to fight along side those men whose lives he was trying to save through this bold strategy of the Dardanelles. The crisis over the Dardanelles weaken fatally the position of Herbert Asquith as Prime Minister, and he was replaced in the aftermath by Churchill's old associate, David Lloyd George, the man who had played such a role in doing Churchill in at the time of the Dardanelles. But it would be LLoyd George, who, in 1917, would call Churchill back into the government. The public outcry—particularly in the press—over the Dardanelles had been such that a Parliamentary committee had investigated it and, finally, all the papers were available through this commission. Churchill's side could be told—he was brought back to report to it, to testify before it, and when the commission was finished, Churchill was completely cleared. It was absolutely certain, the commission said, that the entire Cabinet had been involved, had wanted to go ahead with the Dardanelles, that the chiefs of staff had been in favor of the campaign, that Churchill himself was not to be blamed. But you know, years later, people would still shout out at Churchill as he was giving a speech: how about the Dardanelles? The newspapers would always bring up the Dardanelles as an example of his folly years later. In fact, when the Allies were working closely with Churchill, when the Americans were, during the Second World War, the Dardanelles and the perception of the Dardanelles was a primary reason why Roosevelt and George Marshall, in particular, were highly skeptical of Churchill's strategic ideas and suggestions.

So, it lingered on. Why, why does a lie so frequently triumph over the truth? Churchill said, "Slander moves in six-league boots," and it does. Don't say, where there is smoke, there is fire. President Kennedy said, "Where there is smoke, there is a smoke machine." Nobody knew better than Adolph Hitler that if you want to slander somebody, you tell the absolute opposite of the truth—you don't build upon a little kernel of truth—you tell the absolute opposite. So, this slander about the Dardanelles stuck to Churchill.

But LLoyd George knew Churchill, and LLoyd George had a problem and that is with the administration of the armaments—that was another public outcry. Generals claimed that offenses failed because there were not sufficient shells. LLoyd George wanted somebody in charge of munitions who would make sure the shells got there, and he knew what so many other Cabinet members refused to admit: Churchill was an extremely good administrator—he got jobs done. So, against great criticism and tremendous resistance from fellow Cabinet members, the Prime Minister, LLoyd George, brought Churchill back and made him Minister of Munitions. Churchill immediately took a chaotic organization, divided into 50 different bureaus, reorganized them into 12 bureaus and put businessmen in charge of each of these bureaus, and they got the job done. The troops began to have more than enough shells. Churchill could also go back to one of his favorite ideas, the tank.

In 1914, looking at the western front, the huge line of trenches stretching from the North Sea down to Switzerland, the lunar landscape with barbwire—how could you get across it? Surely there must be a way of building some kind of armored car that could move across that land and the men could follow behind it. Let the armored car punch holes in the barbwire, blow up the machine guns of the Germans. So he began, in 1915, while he was First Lord of Admiralty to develop an idea that was suggested by several people of what we would call today a tank, an armored car. But it couldn't be on wheels because those could not get over all the shell holes and trenches, so it had to work like a tractor, and so it would be put on these treads. Churchill wanted to keep it secret. So, he put out that these men were working on water tanks to be carried to the Middle East, and so it came to be known as the tank. But in the minds of the army, it was Winston's folly, one more crazy idea.

General Haig, who had become a field marshal, who would plan these brilliant campaigns on the Somme and in Passchendaele, knew what you needed to beat the Germans, break through their center, and have them send cavalry. Well, it was what Marlborough had done at Blenheim—let's send cavalry—and he always kept huge quantities of cavalry in reserve knowing that sooner or later they were going to be needed, so don't tell him about tanks. Sure enough, as soon as Churchill had to step down from the Admiralty, the first thing his successor did was dismantle the tank project, and so there it lay. Two tanks were made and Haig was under some pressure to try them; so he did in a way he knew would make them absolutely useless, make them fail; so he could say, see, I told you so.

But as soon as he was back in charge of munitions, Churchill went back with his tanks. By the time the war ended, the tank had proved its value. You must realize the German collapse came very, very rapidly. In March of 1918, the Germans seemed about to take Paris. It was only in August that their forces began to suffer severe reverses. And it was only with the arrival of a large number of American troops and the American offensive in the Argonne in September and October of 1918 that the Germans collapsed. So 1919 was supposed to be a big year for the war and Churchill had put together an enormous array of forces, tanks, as well as making sure there were plenty of aircraft, because he had understood the role that they would play.

So, as Minister of Munitions, he got the job done, did it well. When the war came to an end, Churchill, with his wife, walked through the cheering streets of London—victory had been won! He held no animosity towards the Germans—that valiant disciplined and ruthless race, as he called them. He would write admiringly they succeeded on every front, their science invented terrible mechanisms of death, but is it not enough for all time, Germans, is it not enough? In war, he said, "Let us be resolute in defeat, defiant; in victory, let us have magnanimous feelings." So, he stretched out his hands to the Germans. And so successful was he as Minister of Munitions that LLoyd George then made him, in 1919, Minister for War and Air.

Churchill's first problem was how to demobilize this vast army, because the men wanted to go home, they wanted to go home fast. His predecessor developed this very elaborate system, but the basics of it were that if you had a job waiting for you at home, you were demobilized. So, if you had been in for two days, and had a job waiting for you at home, you got to go home. This did not sit well with people who had been there since 1914. So Churchill came in and set up the very simple procedure: you served the longest, you go home first. He said it was the best thing I ever did. That shows again his care for the ordinary person. Don't you see? These were real men who wanted to get back to their families, and so he saw that it was done.

Now, his task was simple one in the view of the chiefs of staff of the British military establishment; there would not be another war; the Germans were defeated, battered and there would not be another war. So, the budget should be used in other ways, and he had the assignment—and he carried it out—to cut the military budget. This meant cutting the air force, and he did it—that was his task. He had other tasks as well, and one of them, which would once again prove to so many people how reckless he was, he could recommend the troops that remained in the army were to be sent around the empire, where they should go. In the view of the army, he should only carried out their recommendations. Nonetheless, it gave him a certain entrée, and he used that entrée in the Cabinet to say, let's send troops to Russia.

The year is 1919; the Bolshevik Revolution is in full swing. From the outset, Winston Churchill recognized the evil of communism. It is not an alternative economic system. It rests upon the denial of the most fundamental of human rights—the right to property. Can you not understand that? It is not socialism of the variety of our emerging Labour Party. It is a brutal tyranny. He would write of Trotsky and of Stalin that Trotsky was superior to Stalin in intellect, but not in crime. They were both gangsters, and Lenin was the chief gangster. The baboonery of Bolshevism. There are armies fighting against it. There are armies led by Russian generals, who, if we supply them with munitions, and if we send a small critical mass of men, can over through the Bolsheviks; they are just hanging on by a thread—and they were. The Cabinet wanted nothing to do with this; the British public wanted nothing to do with it. We had just fought the most terrible war in history, what sane person wants to involve us in more wars? Winston Churchill is running amuck again. He is a warmonger. He thrives upon war and he wants to get us in a war with Russia. What can we do in the vast steppes of Russia? Let the Russians sort out their own problems. But don't you see? Churchill understood that that form of isolationism ultimately fails. If you allow evil to entrench itself in one country, then it will come back to you.

The Bolsheviks were slaughtering thousands of people. Don't you know they dragged the young officer cadets into the ballroom of the Winter Palace and they raised up the lid of grand piano and put their heads under them and smashed them one by one like walnuts? That is what they are doing. They are allowing people to starve to death. Don't you know they are saying kill all the Bourgeois? But Comrade Lenin, who was bourgeois, why look in his soup pot and if he has a bit of meat in there shoot him. That is a bourgeois. They are killing people for just who they are. But, it fell upon deaf ears and once again it cost him much of his political capital. The newspapers hounded him and the government ultimately did nothing. The White Armies, the armies against the Bolsheviks, would fade away and communism would be entrenched. It also cost him much credit with British labor because the British Labour Party, and many British working people, saw this as the great fight for the workingman—that this was communism. It was being established and here was Winston Churchill trying to hold it down, just the way he was trying to hold down the labor man. They could not look into the future to see all the horrors. This was a workers' state being created. Besides, some of the finest British intellectuals said how wonderful Bolshevism was. I have been to the future, one said, and it works.

But, he had proved his value as Secretary for War and Air, and, in 1921, he was made Colonial Secretary. That LLoyd George was a clever fellow, because I am telling you if there was one really hard ministry in 1921, it was the Colonial Secretary. Not only did he have responsibilities for the whole of the empire—and we must remember that the British Empire reached its height after the First World War, the break up of the Ottoman Empire, the Turkish Empire, gave it mandates under the League of Nations in the Middle East, in Palestine, in Iraq—and LLoyd George also saw to it that the duties of Churchill included Ireland and the Irish problem. So, Churchill had two problems, two issues that are still with us so much today: Ireland and the Middle East.

Churchill went out to the Middle East taking with him as an advisor, T. E. Lawrence, Lawrence of Arabia. They were two men made for each other—men of bravery and valor. Lawrence admired Churchill, and Churchill looked upon Lawrence as one of the grandest men he had ever met. There is nothing he couldn't do if he set his mind to it, Churchill said of Lawrence. You see, Churchill was a truly great man, and he was not threatened by excellence; he wanted excellence around him. He takes Lawrence out even though they don't see eye to eye on the Middle East. Lawrence believes that Britain has very strong commitments to the Arabs and these would not include a Jewish state. But Churchill, for a long time already, had been, as he would say later, a Zionist. He believed in a homeland for the Jews, and he believed this must be carved out of Palestine. He understood that this might involve the taking away of land from the Arabs and, as always, he set priorities. He said, how do I judge this? I say, Look what the Jews have done in Palestine; look how they have begun to create a garden out of the desert. He was a close friend of the leading Zionist leaders, and he worked closely with them. He was not popular in countries of the Middle East. In Egypt he was booed. When he went to Jerusalem there were threats upon his life. He believed that the British had committed themselves, in 1917, through the Balfour Declaration, to the establishment of the Jewish homeland. He worked his best to set it in motion. He was opposed by major figures in the government; he was opposed by the army who put great confidence in the Arab soldiers and in using Arab troops in defense of the empire. But he clung to this belief. He planted a little tree at what would become the Hebrew University. The little tree, when he was handed it to plant, was broken, it could not live; he asked for another and planted it. Never give up, he said. So, in 1948, in addressing a Jewish group, he said, "I stood with you through the darkest days, when many of the leading men in England were opposed to a Jewish state, I am not about to abandon you now in your hour of glory."

Then there was Ireland, a torn and unhappy land—just as it is today. But all of it then was under British rule. Queen Victoria had said (and many agreed), "I do not think we should give away what is ours." So all through the later part of the 19th century, the question of home rule had been a violent issue in British politics. The great Prime Minister Gladstone fell from power for endorsing Irish home rule: the idea that the Irish govern their internal affairs and a part of the empire for military defense in foreign policy. As Minister of War, Churchill had sent troops to Ireland. Already, in 1916, there had been a terrible uprising in Ireland during the war, the Easter Rebellion. Then, after the war was over, bloodshed on a terrible scale throughout Ireland, political assassinations. Churchill sent troops who had mustered out of the army. They wore black hats, and they had a brown belt and their khaki uniforms on—they were called the Blacks and Tans, and they shot people dead. The IRA was a terrorist branch and the Blacks and Tans shot them dead—an armed warfare went on. Now, in his role as Colonial Secretary, Churchill was given the task of trying to negotiate some kind or arrangement. On the one hand there were the British unionists, like Sir Henry Wilton, a brave soldier, and utterly committed that all of Ireland would remain British. It was just that simple. It would never be an independent country; it was British just as much as Scotland was; it was part of Britain. On the other hand, the IRA and the Irish Republicans demanded all of Ireland free and independent—a Republic of Ireland. There would be no compromise.

Churchill sought to bring them together, and he began negotiating with one of the most unlikely of characters, Michael Collins, an IRA gunman. He hated Churchill. He hated what Churchill stood for, hated Churchill for bringing in the Blacks and Tans, knew about Churchill's father who had said, "Remember Ulster will fight, and Ulster will be right. The northern counties will fight to keep all of Ireland part of Britain and they would be right to do so." And there was a price, there was a bounty on the head of Michael Collins, a huge bounty. Yet Churchill said come to London, talk with me, come under armistice, and they met. Collins was a bulldog man like Churchill; they looked very much alike, though he had more hair than Churchill. Collins just glowered at him, and Churchill said, I hear they have a huge bounty on your head. Collins said, yes, don't you think you put it there? And Churchill said, yes I did, but let me show you something. He pulled out the poster that the Boers had put on him, 25 pounds, and he said, look, that is all the Boers thought I was worth, see how much more admiration I have for you? And Collins stuck out his hand and they shook hands. They began to negotiate, bringing others in with them. The only possible compromise was what we still have today: that the seven northern counties, Northern Ireland, Ulster, would remain part of Britain and a free state would be established for the rest of Ireland. It would control its own government, with its own Parliament, but be part of the empire and follow British foreign policy. It was a halfway house and Ireland could then develop it, as it would do, into a free republic. You will recall that in World War II, Ireland was neutral—this was the halfway house. So, the agreement was signed on December 6, 1921. Churchill and other British ministers, as they signed it, said, this could be our political death warrant, so strongly is the feeling against establishing Ireland as a free state in Parliament, particularly in the Conservative Party. Michael Collins said, this is my actual death warrant, and so it would be; he would be shot dead a few months later by IRA gunmen believing that he had betrayed the cause of Ireland. So much resistance was there among the Irish Republicans that battle broke out in Dublin, and Churchill asked the question: Is Michael Collins still alive, if you assault the positions in Dublin, are there men who will die for the Irish free state? That is ultimately the question, and there were, and one of them would ultimately be Michael Collins himself.

But as an extraordinarily difficult, volatile problem, again the smart politician would have said, Prime Minister I don't want to be Colonial Secretary any more, I don't want to be in charge of Ireland. That was a sure way to political disaster, but it had to be done. The Irish are an ancient race; they are a parent nation; many of the greatest countries of the world, they have fought with valor on field after field under our Union Jack, let them go, be worthy. So, ultimately, both in the Middle East and in Ireland, for good or ill, Churchill, as a statesman, laid the foundations that still exist today.

This is an extraordinary man with already an extraordinary career. In 1922, over a small incident in the Middle East, in Turkey as a matter of fact, the government of LLoyd George fell and the Liberal Party was out. Once again, Churchill was blamed for this small incident. It was a little fortress city called Chanak. The Turks were demanding to take it. There were British troops there. Remember, the Turkish empire had been divided up under the great Kemal. The Turks were re-establishing their country; they were determined to drive out all foreign troops; they had driven out the Greeks; they had driven out the French; and they were going to drive the British out. They were attacking the small fortress, and the Cabinet was all in a dither: What are we going to do? We don't have the allies to support us in this, and the soldiers don't want to fight. Churchill said, beat the Turks and then give them the city, but don't surrender without fighting. That warmonger again, and sure enough, the press picked it up, the government collapsed. Churchill did it, don't you see, he got us in trouble again with his warmongering. No, it is that you should always negotiate from strength.

The government fell and Churchill had to run again for Parliament. He was going to run from his seat that he had held for so many years, Dundee in Scotland. Dundee was a very working class city and a lot of people were out of jobs after the First World War and the ending of the armaments industry, ship building. They were poor, they were depressed, and they wanted little part of Churchill. The campaign was going to be difficult. In 1922, at the critical moment, when he was about to roll into his campaign at full speed, he had appendicitis and was in bed. So, Mrs. Churchill, who had just had a baby, went up there and the crowds spit on her. Well, she wore pearls and things like that. But they spit on her, and they rocked her car when she tried to drive away. Winston Churchill came up out of his sick bed, and if you have ever had an appendectomy, it hurts for about two weeks, it is very painful. He was brought up there and tried to sit and give a speech, and they yelled at him, how about the Dardanelles? The Dardanelles could have saved thousands of lives, I glory in the Dardanelles, Churchill replied. Warmonger, they yelled. How about shooting down minors? You want to shoot us down, they shouted out. He lost, and tragically of all, he lost to a prohibitionist—somebody in favor of outlawing whiskey.

It was the most terrible thing he could imagine. I woke, he said, to find myself without a seat, without a party, without an appendix. So, indeed the old Liberal Party had all but collapsed. British politics had become far more polarized, the Conservative Party, now the Labour Party. The Labour Party was bent upon a socialist program. They had begun as a small branch of the Liberal Party, the labor committee, but they had now become a major force in British politics. For the old liberal point of view, based on free trade and helping to get welfare benefits, there was increasingly little room in the British world. From 1922 to 1924, Churchill would loose two more elections. He would be out of Parliament that whole time. Also, he would suffer the crushing blow of the death of his little daughter Marigold, the "Duckadilly." Just a toddler, she caught what was thought to be strep throat, it turned into meningitis, and she died. Churchill's wife gave a cry like a wounded animal and never fully recovered, a terrible blow.

In 1924, he stood again under the title that was really his, an independent constitutionalist, and was elected. And then, with the Liberal Party collapsing, he joined the Conservative Party again. He further alienated people in the Liberal Party and made people in the Conservative Party think he was nothing but a political opportunist. And what opportunity he got, because he now was made by the new Prime Minister, Stanley Baldwin, Chancellor of the Exchequer, the very office his father had once held. He still had the robes that had been his fathers. Chancellor of the Exchequer, Secretary of the Treasury, was thought to be the most important positions leading to the Prime Ministership—it was the stepping-stone. When Lord Randolph had fallen from his position as Chancellor of the Exchequer, a very presumptuous young man showed up at the door of Lady Randolph and said, I want the robes of office. She said, I am keeping them for my son. Sure enough, he would wear those robes. For five years, matching the term of office of great figures like Pitt, he would serve as Chancellor of the Exchequer. He would follow the advice of leading experts of the time and take Britain back on to the gold standard. His speeches were a masterpiece, holed in the Parliament for two and a half to three hours, going over budgetary figures. Stanley Baldwin would write at the end of one of them, "I don't like to use the word 'brilliant.' It sounds too much like brilliantine to me, the stuff you stick your hair down with. But if I may use it in its pristine sense, your speech was brilliant. I want to shake your hands with both of mine." So, once again it seems the peak was in sight and all of his talents, and energy, and genius could serve his country at the highest level.

©2001 The Teaching Company.

# Lecture Seven
# In the Wilderness

**Scope:**

Britain was given little chance to recover from World War I. The 1920s saw a devastating general strike and a stock market crash. In 1925, Churchill rejoined the Conservative Party and, as Chancellor of the Exchequer, reinstated the gold standard. When the Labour Party took over the government in 1929, Churchill was out of office and out of favor in his own Conservative Party. He entered what was termed "the wilderness." He took refuge at his country home of Chartwell. Here, we encounter Churchill as a faithful husband and devoted father. We experience his love of life and hobbies. We see him as a multifaceted genius, painter, and author, who earned much of his livelihood through his writings. This time was a period of renewal, enabling Churchill to rally a nation "never to surrender."

## Outline

I. After World War I, the Conservative Stanley Baldwin became Prime Minister.

    **A.** Britain, under Baldwin, wanted to get back to normal.

    **B.** The working man wanted benefits; labor was restless.

    **C.** From 1922 to 1924, Churchill lost three elections and was out of Parliament during this time.

    **D.** Smarter politicians adapted their political speeches in the elections of 1922–1924 to accommodate the leftward move of the British electorate. By contrast, Churchill spoke out boldly against the evils of socialism.

    **E.** In 1924, he was elected to Parliament from the town of Epping, supported by the Conservative Party. He held this seat until 1964.

    **F.** After the Labour, or Socialist, Party replaced the Liberal Party as the only real alternative to the Conservative Party, Churchill rejoined the Conservative Party in 1925 and became Chancellor of the Exchequer.

    **G.** In May 1926, a general strike broke out across Britain in sympathy with the miners, whose wages had been cut.

**H.** Many ordinary people tried to run the country in place of those on strike.

**I.** Baldwin gave Churchill the task of issuing a newspaper.

**J.** Churchill published the *British Gazette* for eight days.

**K.** Each issue came out with virulent attacks on labor.

**L.** When the strike came to an end, Churchill, as Chancellor of the Exchequer, and with the support of the Bank of England, put Britain back on the gold standard.

**II.** In 1929, the Conservative government yielded to a Labour government.

    **A.** Ramsey MacDonald was the new Prime Minister.

    **B.** The stock market crash of 1929 cost Churchill a considerable fortune, threatening his financial security and that of his family.

    **C.** In 1931, Churchill broke with the leadership of the Conservative Party on the question of ultimate independence for India.

    **D.** He remained in Parliament, but in British political language he had "entered the wilderness"—he was out of favor with his own party.

    **E.** Most astute observers believed that Churchill's political career was finished.

**III.** The most important figure in Churchill's life was his wife, Clementine.

    **A.** Clementine was the granddaughter of the Countess of Airlie.

        **1.** Her family was highly respectable but not wealthy.

        **2.** She was educated at the Sorbonne and liberal in her political views.

        **3.** She was strong willed and shrewd and gave Churchill good advice.

        **4.** Churchill was devoted and faithful to her through 57 years of marriage.

    **B.** Clementine and Winston had four daughters and one son: Diana, Randolph, Sarah, Marigold, and Mary. Marigold died in early childhood.

    **C.** Churchill was a loving and generous father. The children were devoted to him.

©2001 The Teaching Company.

**IV.** In the 1930s, a period Churchill called "the wilderness," Churchill took refuge in his home at Chartwell, a mansion dating back to 1086.

    **A.** In 1922, the year Churchill's mother died, Churchill bought a mansion called Chartwell.

    **B.** Chartwell would be Churchill's home until his death in 1965.

        **1.** The attention Churchill lavished on Chartwell made it a statement of his own personality.

        **2.** He lived expansively, if not extravagantly.

        **3.** Servants were an accepted part of his life.

        **4.** He ate simple food with vigor.

        **5.** He enjoyed good wine, liquor, and cigars.

    **C.** He enjoyed extending hospitality, and the celebrities of the day were frequent guests at Chartwell.

        **1.** Churchill was emboldened, not threatened, by greatness. He surrounded himself with outstanding people, such as Lawrence of Arabia and Charlie Chaplin.

        **2.** For the same reason, his study was filled with memorabilia of Napoleon.

    **D.** He was a man of enthusiasms, as revealed in his hobbies. Flying, brick laying, pond building, tropical fish, horse racing, and pig farming were among his hobbies at various periods in his life.

**V.** Churchill's primary financial support came from his writings.

    **A.** Much of Churchill's time at Chartwell was spent writing books, articles, and correspondence.

    **B.** By 1940, he had written more than 25 books and over 225 articles. In his lifetime, he wrote 56 books.

    **C.** The quality of his work is demonstrated by the fact that he won the Nobel Prize for Literature in 1953.

    **D.** His literary output was facilitated by the use of research assistants and his practice of composing by dictation.

    **E.** His income from his writings was frequently in excess of a million dollars, reckoned in today's values.

    **F.** The subjects of his books and articles reveal his multifaceted genius, ranging over politics, history, painting, social issues, hobbies, and many other topics.

**G.** He wrote five books that would each be a life work for most academic historians today.

    **1.** *Lord Randolph Churchill*, 2 vols. (1906).

    **2.** *The World Crisis*, 6 vols. (1923–1931).

    **3.** *Marlborough, His Life and Times*, 4 vols. (1933–1938).

    **4.** *A History of the English-Speaking Peoples*, 4 vols. (1956–1958).

    **5.** *The Second World War*, 6 vols. (1948–1953).

**VI.** Painting was more than a hobby for Churchill; it was a vocation.

    **A.** He took up painting seriously as a stress reliever during World War I.

    **B.** His battlefield sketches during the Boer War were published to illustrate his dispatches.

    **C.** Distinguished art critics admired his paintings, many of which came to be hung in galleries and museums.

    **D.** Churchill became an honorary member of the Royal Academy of Art.

    **E.** At one point in his life, he derived a considerable income from his paintings, which were used as the subjects for Hallmark greeting cards.

    **F.** His favorite subjects were landscapes. The colors he chose were bold and bright.

    **G.** He mostly followed the style of the impressionists.

    **H.** Churchill's paintings, which number in the hundreds, reflect a profound optimism about life.

## Essential Reading:

Churchill, *Painting as a Pastime*.

James, *Churchill*, pp. 150–197.

Manchester, *Churchill*, volume I, pp. 736–883; *Churchill*, volume II, pp. 3–37.

## Supplementary Reading:

Ashley, *Churchill as Historian*.

Soames, *Winston and Clementine*; *Churchill, His Life as a Painter*.

**Questions to Consider:**

1. Do you think a politician's personal life should have any bearing on his political reputation?

2. Do you think it the test of greatness in a leader that he or she does not feel threatened by greatness in others?

# Lecture Seven—Transcript
## In the Wilderness

In our last lecture, we looked at Winston Churchill in the 1920s, the period following the First World War, and we saw how in the last half of the that decade he came back into considerable political power, holding the office of Chancellor of the Exchequer, the Treasury Secretary, and rejoin the Conservative Party. He was much in favor with the Prime Minister, Stanley Baldwin, who looked upon Churchill at this point as a possible successor. Baldwin was a man very different from Churchill: he defined the term mediocrity; he was a political placebo. If Churchill's signatory later on would be holding up his sign in a "V" for victory, Baldwin is simply holding up a his finger to test the wind. But he understood the mood of the nation and Churchill would later write: "A Prime Minister must represent the mood of the nation."

This was a Britain that wanted to get back to normal after the war, it was a Britain in which the working man wanted benefits, and Baldwin was eager to give them in order to maintain votes. It was a Britain that did not want to think about war. The "Dear Vicar" (as he was called by many), Stanley Baldwin, simply exuded the sense of confidence, well-fed normalcy. He, in fact, was very well educated. He had that classical education that Churchill did not have. He was a president of the British Classical Association. He read Greek and Latin for pleasure, made speeches on the value of learning the classics and how important they were. Well educated, lazy, he was very good at delegating authority and found in Churchill a very eager beaver, eager worker.

But things were not simple in this first Conservative government under Stanley Baldwin. Labor was very restive and, in fact, in May of 1926, a general strike broke out. The miners were being ground down by their bosses. It was difficult for Britain's coal industry to regain its position or world dominance. Its equipped was out molded, and the way that the bosses saw to do it was simply to cut the minor's wages; they were already miserable enough. In sympathy with the miners, the whole British labor force, under its labor unions, went on a general strike starting on May 3. Everything shut down—no railroads, no buses—nothing was in operation, and it was a great danger of course to the public welfare. Many ordinary people,

©2001 The Teaching Company.

middle-class people, took up the task of running buses and being train conductors, trying to keep things going.

It was a desperate situation and Baldwin was wise enough to know that Churchill would just make more trouble. How could he keep Churchill from being too actively involved, making labor even more angry? So, he gave Churchill the task of issuing a newspaper, because the newspapers were on strike too and all these wild rumors were circulated through Britain. So Churchill began to bring out some thing called the *British Gazette*. For eight days it came out, the workers were pressed into service, coming from all kinds of trades, and Churchill had them working. One time he said, have you got enough beer in here? And they said yes. He said you could never have enough and gave them a pound note. Each issue came out with these virulent attacks upon labor and the damage they were doing to the public; they were written by Churchill, no doubt about that. For eight days it went on, until finally, the general strike came to an end. Baldwin said, One of the cleverest things I ever did was put Winston Churchill in charge of that paper. It allowed him to run his mouth off as much as he wanted to and yet do no damage. When the strike was over, and Parliament was meeting to discuss the issue—and the Labour Party was still very angry about it—Churchill got up and said, let me tell you, if you ever dare unleash upon the British public another general strike, then I shall unleash upon you. And there were shouts: warmonger! Dardanelles! Another *British Gazette*! They just broke up with howls.

He put Britain, as we saw in our last lecture, back up on the gold standard. Now, this is what the best advisors told him to do, his predecessors. Chancellor of the Exchequer was bound to do that, that was the policy that the government had insisted upon; the Bank of England's director insisted upon it, and so England went back up on the gold standard.

In 1929, a new election was held, a general election, in the spring of that year. Things were booming pretty much in England at that time, and when people are prosperous, they think they wanted a change. So, the Conservative government was swept out and the Labour Party became the dominant force in Parliament. Ramsey MacDonald became the new Prime Minister. Stanley Baldwin was also lucky nothing ever stuck to him. He got out of office right before, of course, the Great Depression, which came in the fall of 1929. But

Churchill was now out of office, and he, in fact, would stay out of office for the next decade, though none could foresee it at the moment. That same year, while he was traveling across the United States in the summer and early fall, traveling with his son on a private railroad car that had been lent to him by one of his admirers, the great stock market crash occurred. As he sailed over, he wrote a letter back to his wife saying how wonderful financial security is— my stocks are just booming in America, and now that I out of office I can write; I can do the things I want to without worrying for a living. He was wiped out in the stock market crash—another terrible blow.

He came back and settled in—still a member of Parliament, but out of office—settled in to his life at Chartwell. Within a year he had broken with the Conservative Party leadership—remaining a member but broken with the leadership—and broken bitterly with Stanley Baldwin over the Conservative Party's desire to see India receive ultimate independence. In these years, all through the '30s, Churchill was said to be "in the wilderness"—out of favor with his party, out of office. Chartwell, his home in the south of England, in Kent, would be his castle, his place of refuge. There we see Churchill as a man, a full rounded human being, so very different from the titanic and evil figures of Stalin and Hitler. Chartwell remains today as it was in Churchill's time. You can walk through the rooms, see the very furniture, and picture Churchill there as we want to do in this lecture.

His mother had died in 1922. They had grown quite close. She had married two more times, always to men much younger than herself. She was wearing a new pair of Italian high heels and she stumbled and fell down the steps, broke her leg so badly it had to be amputated. She died of complications following that, but they had grown close. The real figure in his life, from 1908 onward, was his wife, Clementine, "Clemmie," Clementine Hosier. She came from an aristocratic family. She was the granddaughter of the Countess of Airlie. But her father, Mr. Hosier, was a bit of a bounder. He refused to have sex with his wife. Clementine used to ponder in later years who her father might actually have been. He made quite a fortune in the financial district of London, but would not support the family, so they grew up in fairly modest circumstances. Clementine, when Churchill met her, was actually a tutor in French. She had studied at the Sorbonne and was beautiful. The first time she met Winston Churchill was in 1904, at a dance, and he came up to her and just

 ©2001 The Teaching Company.

stood there. He said, I was struck silent for once by her beauty. There was this redheaded man standing staring at her, and she got embarrassed. She waved to a man she knew and they danced off together, leaving him there. The man said, why are you talking to that awful wretched Winston Churchill? I wasn't talking to him, is he really that bad? Oh yes, everybody says he is. But they met again four years later, he pursued her with ardor and she married him. He asked her to marry him at Blenheim. He said, I took two great decisions at Blenheim: one to be born and one to be married. I have never regretted either of them.

Through 57 years he was absolutely devoted to her. The letters that they wrote to one another were published by their daughter—what a wonderful glimpse they give into their lives. They had little pet names for each other—not just Clemmie—but she was also "cat," and he was "pug," "amber pug," or "pig." When she was pregnant she would draw these little fat cats at the end of their letters. They would frequently write letters, even when they were home together. My dearest Clemmie...Your very loving Winston. So from the first letter to the very end 57 years later...

She was a very shrewd judge of people, much more shrewd than Winston. She gave him very good advice again and again about politics, and she lived for Winston and their children. The first, Diane, was born in 1909. They weren't sure what she was going to be—a little boy or a little girl—so they caller her, "pup-kitten." And then there was Randolph, born two years later, "Chumbolly"; and then Sara; the sad little Marigold, "Duckadilly," who died; and then Mary, who would become Churchill's dearest daughter of them all. And he loved these children. He would never punish them. If they acted badly, the worst thing he would do is send them out of his sight, but he would never touch them in terms of spanking them. He was loving and devoted as a father above all during these years at Chartwell. It was a home he had bought in 1922. Mrs. Churchill did not want him to buy it, she never liked the house. But she made it a wonderful home for him. He paid 5,000 pounds for it in the currency of the day and spent 20,000 improving it. It was a bit of England. The central part, where he had his study, had been built in 1086, and it had been added on to over the years. So only 20 years after the Battle of Hastings the central part had been built. His study speaks volumes about Churchill; it is filled with the memorabilia of Napoleon. He wanted great men around him, in all things. There he wrote; there he pondered the history of John, Duke of Marlborough. He pondered the history of the English speaking peoples. He wrote his magnificent memoirs from the First World War, *World Crisis.* There he lived, rich and full life, going up to London to give speeches.

There, at Chartwell, he was king. He would wake up in the morning about 8:30 or 9:00 (he always slept with a mask, he would decided when he woke up don't you see, not the sun). He would lie in bed frequently in a very colorful kimono that he had. His breakfast would be brought up to him: bacon, eggs, toast with cherry jam, and then something left over the night before like a steak, three or four slices of roast beef, half of a chicken. And then he would also have his first scotch of the day, and don't let anybody tell you these were weak scotches—they were strong robust scotches, like the cigars he smoked—nine scotches a day and nine cigars a day. There he would lie in bed until noon, doing his correspondence, dictating to his secretaries, reading the newspapers and then get ready for lunch. He was always running late, so about 12:30–12:45 they would draw his bath for him. Now there were 18 servants at Chartwell, and one would draw his bath, and it had to be exactly 98 degrees. He would get in it, and he would have a thermometer put in and it would be raised to exactly 102 degrees. He once remarked quizzically, I don't think I have ever drawn a bath in my life. He would get in there—he was about five foot six, weighted 215 pounds—and would wallow around in the bath, and on more than one occasion would splash out so much water that it would come down through the chandelier in the living room and sprinkle, for example, the French ambassador sitting there. Then he would get dressed, come down, and if it was an ordinary luncheon with the family, he would wear a silk shirt open at the collar, a velvet dressing gown, little black velvet slippers with "WSC" on them embroidered in gold. I am always content, he said, with the very best. And so, hee would have his lunch.

But frequently, there were distinguished guests. Because he was a great man, he wanted great people to come to his lunch: Albert Einstein, Charlie Chaplain, Lawrence of Arabia (who would sometimes, to the delight of the children, wear his full gown as an Arab Shariff. And then there would be lunch, always starting off with a glass or two of champagne. He liked simple food. Good food is just wasted on Winston, Mrs. Churchill said. He liked good red beef, so he would have roast beef, washed down with lots of wine;

then port cheese; and then good old brandy at the end of things, one or two glasses. You may think that is a lot of drinking, but he said, I have taken far more out of alcohol than alcohol is ever taken out of me. Then, he was the center of attention at the conversation. Shut up Randolph, he said. Lie down, stop interrupting my people, he would say to his son. He said, the best thing is a good meal, then a monologue by myself, that is true entertainment.

Then, in the afternoon, he liked to take a nap; he had learned this while in Cuba. He thought an hour nap was a wonderful thing and enabled you to put in two days worth of work. Then, dictating on his books and articles in the afternoon, and feeding his goldfish—that was a part of his day, to go to the ponds he had built with his own hands, there at Chartwell, and feed his gold carp. Off , off, off, he would say, and throw them out some special maggots that he had delivered on a regular basis to feed them. He loved animals. You could go in and watch him working on his proofs with a parakeet on his head, a yellow cat across his stomach, and his little dog Rufus, a poodle, stretched across his feet. On one occasion he was talking to a high government official and Rufus was playing with the phone wire, and Churchill kicked it and said, get off the line, you fool, and the minister hung up immediately. He called him back and said, no, not you.

Now, after his nap and working in the afternoon, he would again have this same kind of meal, drinking two or three scotches in between plenty of wine for the evening meal, which was the grand occasion. Then upstairs about 10:00 to start dictating his books, and his secretary said that is when he seemed most refreshed. He would work on from 10:00 till about 3:00 or 4:00 in the morning, starting off slow and picking up.

He never really learned to pronounce the letter "s." He could not pronounce it as a little boy. The poster that the Boer said about him said: Cannot speak the letter "s." And he still had trouble with it. He mastered it in speeches to Parliament. But when he would dictate, he really couldn't get it down. His secretaries had trouble keeping up with him and you didn't ever stop and say, I didn't quite understand that. Then you would give him back what you had written down, and he said, you missed 10 out of 20 words, you fool, you fool. Then he would apologize, calm back down, and get on with it. But he had a short temper; more than once he would leap out of the bath with an idea, and shout for his secretary, and forget he didn't have any clothes on, and she would run up and then run downstairs screaming. One secretary had it happen to her the first day she was there, and she kept running and never came back.

There was his family, his children, his pets, and then there was his writing. And in this we are talking about what he wrote in 1931 to 1939: eleven books and more than 400 articles. Articles on a range of things, not just political issues, but on sport, on what is the best past time you can have, all matter of issues. Eleven books and more than 400 articles. His book, *Marlborough*, four volumes, would be enough for any tenured professor to do in a lifetime. Richly researched books. He walked about the fields at Blenheim. And he made, in most years, more than a million dollars in our currency. Highest paid journalist of his day. Now, he spent a lot of it, this was a lavish life style that he had, but picture writing that much and earning that much; that is success in the way we define success making money. He was one of the most successful authors of his day.

But perhaps just as revealing is Churchill as a painter. There has been published recently a book by his daughter, Mary, on Churchill as a painter. It is a splendid introduction to his painting, but it is also so filled with love. His daughter just loved him so much it comes through on every page. Could we all be that lucky, to have our children, so many years later, be so devoted to us? She describes how he began painting, and he himself wrote up a fine little article called, "Painting as a Pastime." He said: I began to paint at the time of the Dardanelles, after I had lost my office. I was so depressed I could think of nothing else but painting. It was a change and that, he said, is the key to true relaxation—the change that is the key. Most of us read for one reason or another and work all the time. So reading is not going to do it. But something like painting… I beg you to take it up he says, that unleashes the stress. He said, there I was, depressed on a beautiful Sunday (in their little cottage at the time Hoe Farm, 1915), and there was my sister-in-law, Lady Gwendeline ("Goonie" they called her) and she was painting with watercolors. I said, is that fun? She said, yes, try it; and I did. Mrs. Churchill, seeing that I was taken with it, went out and got me a set of oil paints. I stood there, she put up a canvas for me and reached on my palette took a little bit of blue and dotted it on, but the canvas was so big and so challenging. Then, suddenly there was a motor car and out stepped the wife of a well-known artist, herself an artist, and she said, what are you doing? And he said, I made this little dot. And she said, give me that. She started splashing blue all over—and I said, I can do it. I grabbed it up and I went after that canvas; I slashed it and cut it, and suddenly, it was cowering before me. From that moment on I felt no worry. And so he began to paint.

His paintings would hang ultimately in distinguished museums like the Tate in London. He would never call himself a master artist, but he was a very fine artist. Picasso would say of Churchill, "he could earn his living as a professional painter." Picasso was not an admirer of Churchill the statesman, but he admired his paintings. He learned from others: John Lavery and Hazel Lavery, the woman who first introduced him to painting; Walter Sickert, a well known painter of the day; William Nicholson, much admired by Mrs. Churchill (who had known him as a girl); and Paul Maze, who was perhaps the most influential painter upon Churchill. Maze was born of an English and French mixed marriage. He had served in the English army. He wrote a little book during the First World War called the *Frenchman in Khaki*. He won medals for valor from both the French government and the British government. Churchill admired him as a swash buckling hero, as well as a painter. Mrs. Churchill wasn't that crazy about him, in fact, she generally disliked those swash buckling types, thought they played to a bad element in Winston's character, pushed him on. But he loved Paul Maze, and Maze gave him a great deal of advice on painting.

And then, already by 1921, six years after beginning painting, Churchill was in Paris with a Swiss friend of his, Charles Montage (who was an art critic) and they went to a gallery. Churchill said, I want to take you to a gallery. And he looked and said, what do you think of these paintings by Charles Morin here? And Montage said, well I like them quite a bit. The gallery owner came over and said, I guess we don't know much about Mr. Morin, but we have sold six of his paintings. Well, that was, in fact, Churchill's pseudonym. He was already exhibiting in Paris and selling his paintings. Now, I would call that success.

In 1925, there was an amateur art exhibit in London, and Churchill had submitted one of his paintings, a winter scene at Chartwell. The critics were very distinguished judges: one of them was a well-known sponsor of art; one was Oswald Birley, who was portrait painter of the time; and the other was Kenneth Clark, then a young man who had gone on to be one of the most distinguished art critics of the 20th century. Oswald Birley went first, and was there early, and looked at all the paintings, and picked out this winter scene, thought it looked excellent. These paintings were not signed, you understand. Then, the well known art connoisseur, Mr. DeVane, he looked at them and said, well I agree with you, that is the best one, but this is a professional painter, this is rigged, this is not by an amateur, it is too good. Then, Kenneth Clark came in and said, well I think it is by an amateur, and it is the best. So, Churchill won the 1925 art exhibition of amateur paintings.

As he got famous in the aftermath of the war, he became an honorary member of the Royal Academy, but the mark is there already that he was a good artist and he worked at it. He had a superb studio set up for him at Chartwel, and he painted hundreds of paintings over the years, hundreds of them. Unlike Hitler who claimed to be an artist and never produced any thing, Churchill just quietly worked away. He didn't like to give his paintings away. In fact, the king had to press him to give up a painting to be held for auction, which sold at a very good price. He loved his paintings the way he loved his children, and there were very telling about his character. He followed mostly the style of the impressionists. And in this little work painting, as a past time, he said that they were like Shelley, the literature, after all the classical influence they brought joy in; a sense of life back into painting. He loved bright colors, and he painted landscapes. He said, "When I get to heaven I want to spend the first million years, at least a good part of it, painting. And I think that on my palette there that orange and vermillion will be the dimmest colors and there will be a whole range in new bright colors." You see this optimistic vision of life. One of his earliest paintings is a landscape: a little forest not far from Chartwell, in the sunset, and a mist is falling over it, and there is a single tree sticking up out of the grey, and off in the corner bright lights green and blue and red—the way a sunset is captured there in western England. You always thinks of his famous statement:"In the darkest days of WWII, but look there the sun is bright, the sky is bright."

And so, when he was settling the Near Eastern disputes, when he was working for the establishment of a Jewish state in Palestine, in the midst of crowds shouting at him, he sat down and painted the Pyramids in 1921. It is one of my favorite of his paintings. These monumental structures, rising up under a brilliant sky—orange and blue—and beneath them little tiny figures. How small ultimately is man, and yet how great can his achievements be. A landscape that captured a stream flowing through the Maritime Alps, near the Rivera, shows this mastery of light, glistening upon the water. It was chosen to be exhibited in the Royal Academy in the summer exhibits in 1947. Water, he wrote to Clementine, is so hard to capture; and he worked at it again and again. In 1960, while on active duty at the western front, he painted their little dugout there at "Plug Street" as the British troops called their little village, the shell holes, the damaged church, his comrades sitting around amid shell fire, calmly reading the newspaper, death was such an every day occurrence to them. He loved the Mediterranean, and he loved Morocco.

He took President Roosevelt to a special spot where he liked to paint: a huge canyon with cliffs rising up on either side and he caught them in all their orange majesty, a brilliant blue sky and just a little figure, a few figures running among them—always this theme of the majesty of nature. But my favorite single painting by him, two perhaps, one is portrait of his wife, because he could be a superb portrait painter and he worked from a photograph of her taken 15 years before. He painted it in 1955. She was launching a ship in 1940 and it captures all the gaiety of her smile, the force of her character, and how much he loved her. In 1948, he painted a Buddha, a little Buddha that had been left him by Sir Ian Hamilton. Sir Ian Hamilton, the man at the Dardanelles, the man who had recommended Winston Churchill for a medal of honor, for a Victoria Cross in the South African War. And Ian Hamilton had captured this little Buddha during the Burmese War, so many years before the annexation of Burma, which had been overseen by Lord Randolph Churchill. And there is that black Buddha—silent, inscrutable, and in front of it, Churchill had placed a single brilliant red flower in a vase. The flower will come and go, it will pass away, and the silent Buddha resting there is eternity. It is painted in brilliant colors: solid, clear, luminescent. Churchill is a painter, and insight into the soul of this man so brilliant so well rounded, so gifted, so giving.

# Lecture Eight
## The Nazi Menace

**Scope:**

While Churchill was in the wilderness, Adolf Hitler was achieving the pinnacle of power in Germany. While such politicians as Baldwin and Chamberlain focused on winning elections and balancing budgets, Churchill recognized the evil of Hitler and proclaimed it to an apathetic public. During much of the 1930s, Churchill stood almost alone as he urged Britain to resist Nazi aggrandizement and to prepare for war. This lecture examines the political principles that contrasted Churchill and Hitler and made Churchill regard the Nazi menace with such alarm. Both Hitler and Churchill were men of ambition and patriotism. The difference lay in the moral compass that guided Churchill and that was utterly despised by Adolf Hitler.

## Outline

I. By 1930, many in British political life and in the press thought Churchill's political career was finished. Churchill, too, had thoughts along that line. Hitler rejected an opportunity to meet Churchill for the same reason.

   **A.** In 1930, Churchill published *A Roving Commission: My Early Life*.

   1. He was 56 years old, and this memoir of his life before he entered Parliament reads like the reflection of a man looking back over a career that has closed.

   2. In writing of his father in this book, Churchill seems really to be speaking of himself: "It is never possible for a man to recover his lost position. He may recover another position in the fifties and sixties, but not one he lost in the thirties and forties."

   **B.** Churchill looked his age and frequently dressed in an old-fashioned style.

   **C.** He spoke in old-fashioned phrases; he disliked the use of foreign words and anglicized French words.

   **D.** He wrote in *My Early Life*: "to hold the leadership of a party or a nation with dignity and authority requires that the leader's qualities and message shall meet not only the need but the mood of both."

II. The mood of Britain in 1930 was out of step with Churchill, especially with his grave concern over the rise of German power.

    A. Churchill had warned against Germany's aspirations as early as the 1920s.

    B. But in the aftermath of World War I, Britain did not want to hear about the possibility of another war.

        1. Britain's victory in the First World War had been bought at a price so high as to be almost indistinguishable from defeat.

        2. The British Empire suffered almost one million dead and over three million total casualties.

        3. There was widespread dissatisfaction over the Versailles Peace treaty that ended World War I.

        4. All levels of British society had a general feeling that World War I had been pointless.

        5. There was also the conviction that technology had made warfare so destructive that the next war would destroy civilization.

        6. Patriotism came to be regarded as a false value. In 1933, students at Oxford, potential leaders of the next generation, took an oath never again to fight for king and country—an action that seemed outrageous to Churchill.

        7. Popular culture hammered home the message of the futility of war.

    C. Another casualty of the First World War was the economic power of Britain. The financial base to be a great power had been eroded by the expense of World War I.

    D. These financial difficulties were enormously increased by the worldwide economic depression of 1929 and the 1930s.

    E. The Great Depression of 1929 struck Britain hard and Churchill was blamed for it, because he had put Britain back on the gold standard.

    F. The British Empire was a further casualty. Instead of being viewed as a source of pride and glory, the Empire was seen as a burden that Britain no longer had the strength to bear.

1. The collapse of confidence in Britain as the bearer of civilization made the idea of "the white man's burden" laughable.
2. Even the Conservative Party accepted the idea of ultimate independence for India, "the jewel in the crown" of the British Empire.
G. Churchill was an imperialist, whose warnings of a new war with Germany fell on the ears of a public that was afraid to listen.
H. His incisive wit was not appreciated.
I. Mediocre politicians, such as Stanley Baldwin and Neville Chamberlain, reflected the mood of Britain in the years between World War I and World War II.

III. While Churchill was at the nadir of his political influence, Adolf Hitler was rising to the apex of power in Germany.
A. The background of Hitler was very different from that of Churchill.
B. The similarities between the two men are superficial; the differences, fundamental.
C. Above all, Churchill was guided by a moral compass. He spoke to all that is best in men and women, while Hitler spoke to all that is evil.
D. From the beginning of the rise of Hitler, Churchill recognized him as evil.
E. He read Hitler's book, *Mein Kampf*, as soon as it was translated and realized that Hitler's ideology and political aims, which are openly revealed in the book, posed a serious threat to the world.
F. One of Hitler's first actions was to strip the rights of German Jews.
G. Churchill sought to warn Britain at each critical step in Hitler's plans of European domination, but the British government leaders claimed that Britain should not interfere in another country's internal affairs.
H. Later, Baldwin admitted that he had chosen not to meet the threat of Hitler with firmness for fear of losing the election.

©2001 The Teaching Company.

**I.** The first test case came in 1936 when Germany remilitarized the Rhineland, in violation of the Versailles Treaty. The allies did not respond.

**J.** Baldwin and Chamberlain spoke of a policy of appeasement.

**K.** Meanwhile, Churchill was being provided, at great risk, with confidential information about the size of the British military establishment. The figures were irrefutable that the German airforce was far larger than the British airforce. Yet Baldwin did nothing.

**L.** Also in 1936, Churchill's sense of personal loyalty led him to support the hopeless cause of Edward VIII in the crisis over his marriage to the American Wallis Simpson. For reasons that seem hard to understand today, this dealt a staggering blow to Churchill's political reputation.

**M.** In March 1938, Germany annexed Austria. Churchill was prevented from protesting the move in a newspaper column by Lord Beaverbrook, the newspaper magnate, and the British Broadcasting Corporation would not allow him to broadcast his views.

**N.** In September 1938, Britain and France agreed to Hitler's annexation of the Sudentenland in Czechoslovakia at the Munich Agreement. Chamberlain (who succeeded Baldwin as Prime Minister in 1937) proclaimed "peace in our time."

**O.** Churchill accused the leadership in Parliament of betraying Czechoslovakia and warned that Britain would not escape suffering herself from Hitler's ambitions unless she regained her moral vigor and rearmed.

**Essential Reading:**

Manchester, *Churchill*, volume II, pp. 41–689.

**Supplementary Reading:**

Bullock, *Hitler*.

Charmley, *Churchill*, pp. 2–337.

Churchill, *The Second World War I: The Gathering Storm*, pp. 3–401.

**Questions to Consider:**

1. Do you blame such leaders as Stanley Baldwin and Neville Chamberlain for caring more about balanced budgets and social welfare programs than for military preparedness? After all, should leaders not reflect the will of the voters?

2. Would you agree with some recent historians that Churchill's career until 1940 was "a study in failure"?

 ©2001 The Teaching Company.

# Lecture Eight—Transcript
## The Nazi Menace

In our last lecture, we looked at Winston Churchill at home, at Chartwell. We saw him as an author, as a family man, and as a painter. And it is as a painter that we gain one more insight into the richness of his soul—the very fiber of his being above all—his optimism, that optimism that led him to say, never give up, never, never, never, never weary, never despair, never surrender. We look at these paintings from the 1930s. Paintings when, for example, he is visiting friends on the Rivera, and we see their swimming pools with the villa shimmering in it, reflected. We see magnificent seascapes painted in these bold colors, and we wonder how, within a few years, that will all be shattered, German troops will march and the streets of Paris and Europe will be in danger of falling into a new dark age made even more sinister and protracted by the light of a perverted science. "The gathering storm"—that is what Churchill called it, and that is what he saw long before most statesmen and politicians in Britain were willing to admit it. But by 1930, when Adolph Hitler was still three years from power, Churchill was without influence in Britain and it was generally thought that his career was over.

One of his really great bêtes noires was Nancy Astor. She was an American, Lady Nancy Astor, and had become the first woman member of Parliament. She hated Churchill; she was constantly deriding Churchill. On one occasion, reportedly, they were at a dinner party and Nancy Astor said, if you were my husband, I would put poison in your cup. And Churchill said, yes, if you were my wife, I would drink it. So, she was on a visit to Stalin (she was a great admirer of the Soviet Union) and Stalin said, who are the coming leaders in Britain? This is 1931, and she said, Neville Chamberlain is the coming man. And Stalin said, what about Churchill? And Nancy Astor said, Churchill is finished. So, too, in 1932, when he had an opportunity to meet Churchill, Adolph Hitler refused, saying Churchill is finished.

Churchill may have shared that view in 1930; he was, after all, 56 years old; that is well into middle age. He wrote a book, a wonderful charming book, *My Early Life* (*A Roving Commission: My Early Life*, it is called in America). It is a man looking back over a life that is finished. He would look back upon the fall of his father from power, look back and chuckle about his school days, his time in the army, and writing about his father, but really reflecting upon himself. Churchill says in this book that a man who looses his position in the thirties and forties (that is to say when he is 30 or 40 years old) will never get it back. He may get another position in his fifties and sixties. But the height that he reached in those early years, he can never reclaim. He is talking about himself. He was 56, and he looked it: stoop shouldered we saw; 215 pounds; 5 foot 6. He looked old, bald headed, he was once sitting in the barber's chair and the barber said what kind of hairstyle would you like? Churchill said, a man of my limited resources couldn't afford a hairstyle, just cut. He always wore old-fashioned clothes. He carried a walking stick that had been given to him by King Edward VII, not long after the turn of the century—to my favorite Minister, my youngest minister—was inscribed upon it. He wore a frock coat frequently and carried a huge old-fashioned pocket watch—the turnip, his children called it.

He spoke in old-fashioned phrases. He made Stanley Baldwin, who was quite a classical scholar, wince whenever Churchill pronounced Latin. Churchill said, you have taken away from me the good old Latin, I used to say "vinea vida, vitri" and you want me to say this atrocious "weenie, weenie, wee"; how wrong, how wrong. And he never, for example, would have called it Beijing; it had always been Peking to him. He didn't like words like "pundent," strange words that had been incorporated into our language. He did not like people correcting his pronunciation of French words. He once said to a friend, you like to say you go to "Mar-say," take the train up to "Lee-on," then on to "Parie." I am happy to go to "Mar-sail," stop at "Lions," and go on to "Paris." Out of fashion, out of step.

He also wrote in *My Early Life* that a Prime Minister must reflect not only the need, but the mood of a nation. And the mood of Britain in 1930, and well on into the '30s, was out of step with Winston Churchill, increasingly out of step with his grave concern over the rise of German power. He had seen it early on in the '20s. He had said, I see those sturdy German youth marching, they are looking for weapons, they are determined to overcome this humiliation, they are determined to restore what they see as their national honor, and they will find a leader to make war again. But Britain did not want to hear about war, and it was even more uninterested in war in 1930 than it had been in 1919.

   ©2001 The Teaching Company.

The decade of the '20s brought forth evermore information and facts about how pointless the war had been—how fruitless the slaughter; an entire generation shorn off for nothing. The Versailles Treaty was held to have been a grand failure, imposing upon the Germans impossible payment demands, forcing on the Germans a war guilt clause. We were all equally guilty, and fine minds like John Maynard Keynes denounced the Versailles Treaty. What had the war been for? Nothing, "patriotism" became an outmoded word. At the Oxford Union, where the finest young leaders of a new Britain would be educated, the members took an oath never to fight for king and country. Churchill called it an outrageous statement, but he was heckled down at the Oxford Union as old-fashioned and out-of-step. Leading films and books like *All Quiet on the Western Front* simply hammered home this lesson of the futility of the war. What is more, the war had removed England from its pinnacle of economic power. In economics, as well as politics, victory in the First World War had been bought with a price that made it indistinguishable from defeat. Britain never recovered from the economic disaster of the First World War. The Great Depression of 1929 struck hard at Britain, and once again it was Churchill who took part of the blame. He was blamed for having put Britain up on the gold standard, and it was said that he was responsible for the Great Depression.

Then, the empire, it was no longer a source of pride, but to many British, just a burden. The idea of the "Land of Hope and Glory," the hymn that we looked at in an earlier lecture, had faded. The idea that the British were bringing civilization and liberty to the world had become laughable in the minds of a new generation. The empire was something to be gotten rid of, starting with India. The Conservative Party, as well as the Liberal Party, they both worked assiduously to grant dominion status, looking forward to full independence for India. It was another view with which Churchill was much out of step. So, he would come to Parliament, he would speak out against the proposal to give dominion status to India, only showing how far removed he was from the tempo of the time. He continued to make enemies. He continued to speak with venom and sarcasm. On one occasion, speaking of Ramsey MacDonald, in the early 1930s, then Prime Minister, although working closely with Stanley Baldwin, Churchill spoke of Ramsey MacDonald and said:

> It is amazing how he can take policies, fall after fall, and always get up, his hair a little out of place, but smiling.

When I was a boy [and Mrs. Churchill had urged him not to put this following into his speech], I was taken to see the Barnham Circus, and among the exhibits of monstrosities and freaks was the boneless wonder. I said, "I want to go see that," but I was told it would upset my youthful nervous system. And so I have waited 50 years to see, sitting as Prime Minister, the boneless wonder.

Now that did not gain him friends.

On November 11, 1918, Churchill walked hand in hand with Mrs. Churchill through cheering crowds—victory had been won. That same day in Germany lying in a hospital bed was a corporal; he had been blinded in the gas attack. And as he lay there, the chaplain came in and gave the news that Germany had surrendered. How could this be possible—Adolph Hitler said—we had been on the verge of winning, and with that my whole world crumbled, and I swore an oath, there in that hospital bed, that I would avenge this crime against my country and that I would devote my life to the overthrow of the November criminals, to the Jews and socialists who stabbed our nation in the back.

You cannot image two men more different than Churchill and Adolph Hitler. Hitler had been born April 20, 1889 in circumstances very different from those of Churchill—not in poverty, as he liked to claim later, he was after all the master of the lie—but in perfectly comfortable surroundings. His father had been a customs officer in the Austro-Hungarian Empire, had retired, kept bees in the countryside, and had a perfectly reasonable pension. Hitler's mother doted upon him. Like Churchill, he did very badly in school. He would say (putting it into our terms), show me a boy with a 4.0 GPA and in ten years I will show you a failure. All teachers want to do is turn you into carbon copies of themselves. And again in our terms, if they could do anything they would do, they wouldn't be teachers. So, he despised learning. He was smart enough, and the teachers said if he would discipline himself—doesn't that sound familiar to Churchill's teachers—if he would discipline himself, he could accomplish something. And he wanted to be an artist, Churchill came to painting late, Hitler wanted to be an artist from his teenage years, but he couldn't get into the art academy there in Vienna. I think not because he was a bad painter, some of his paintings from these early years still exist, and they are not bad. But he did not have

©2001 The Teaching Company.

a diploma from high school. He had no connections so he couldn't get in.

While Churchill was serving as First Lord of Admiralty, Adolph Hitler was tramping the streets, first of Vienna, then of Munich, bringing into himself what Churchill would later describe as those "soul destroying hatreds," building up a hatred against the Jews, the socialists, imbibing the racism of Vienna in those years, developing an absurd pride in his Germaness. Then, the First World War came about—it was a tremendous liberation for him. We have a picture interestingly enough, a photograph, not taken intentionally of Hitler at all, but of Hitler throwing his hat up into the air when war is declared. And he is there in Munich. He served with gallantry during the First World War, winning the iron cross, only to see this world collapse and to set out on this course of rebuilding Germany.

Now, Churchill spoke to all that was best in men and women. But there is that other side, men and women are evil as well as good, and Hitler spoke to all that evil—to the malice, the suspicion, the treachery that lurks in human nature. And Germany of the 1920s and early '30s provided the most fertile of breeding grounds: it was a nation that felt itself stripped of honor, reduced to a meager army, no air force, no fleet, forced to accept blame for the First World War, burdened with reparations, and without any confidence in the government that had been imposed upon it. Churchill said, at the time of Versailles, "Let the Kaiser stay on his throne, that will give a focal point," but this was stripped away.

Political party after party, falling and rising with governments, and utter lack of faith in democracy, and then crippled economically, first by huge inflation that destroyed the savings of the middle class and then by a depression equaled only by the depression in the United States. There Hitler flourished, he said the same theme over and over again: it is the fault of the Jews; it is the fault of the socialists. He knew that the way to win the hearts of men and women was by telling the biggest lie possible, and you know, he said all of this openly. He had been arrested after a failed attempt in 1923 to overthrow the government, and he used his trial not to apologize but to speak out openly—heads will roll, Germany will be avenged—and his brief prison term was sort of a celebration, receiving packages, running around in his Lederhosen, and later writing a book, *Mein Kampf, My Struggle*. The world for him was an unceasing struggle, and the purity of the race was what mattered—the strong race won out and others were meant to be dominated, and that race must be pure. To Hitler the Jews were the greatest defilers of the race. He said, we must find our room in the east; we must first win back our honor by conquering France and expand out into the east. Well, Churchill read this book as soon as it was translated into English (he never learned German, I will not learn their beastly language until the Kaiser marches upon London, he once said). But he read it in an English translation, and he understood this man means it.

He followed the rise of Hitler, and when Hitler became Chancellor in January 1933, and when one of his first actions was to strip the civic rights of Germans who were Jewish, strip them away, Churchill said, you cannot allow one group of people to be stripped of their rights without it coming home to you. But you see the easy thing to say, always, we hear it again, is we should not interfere in another country's internal affairs. Well, that is immoral, that is wrong, you cannot allow evil to be done anywhere, and Churchill spoke out. He would later say that the Second World War ought to be called the "unnecessary war." No war would have been easier to stop. If only the threat of Hitler with firmness, but that is the very thing that Stanley Baldwin, and later Neville Chamberlain, did not have; they did not have firmness, and they wanted to suit the mood of the British people. Stanley Baldwin would say, in an a statement that Churchill said was the most shocking he had ever heard in his long Parliamentary career, at a time when the threat was growing obvious, in 1936 Stanley Baldwin said, "If, in 1935, I had been talking to Parliament about rearming, and the danger of war, and increased military spending, that would be the easiest way to have lost the election." What an abdication of responsibility to allow the military of Britain to be threatened because you are afraid of loosing an election? You lead, you don't follow, Churchill said, but no one was really following him in the 1930s.

The first test case really came in 1936. Hitler had begun almost immediately to rearm Germany. The German armed forces, the *Wehrmacht*, was supposed to stay at 100, 000 by the Treaty of Versailles. It was obvious by 1935 it was being expanded and was well over a million. The Germans were not supposed to have a military air force, but they had one. This was an obvious breach of the Versailles Treaty, and by that treaty the French and British could have marched into Germany and removed Hitler; they did not—why

            ©2001 The Teaching Company.

shouldn't the Germans have an army, we have one, let them have one. Then, on March 7, 1936, German troops moved into the Rhineland, that area that has cities like Cologne, and Bohn—by the Versailles Treaty it was demilitarized. The Germans could not have forces there—they could not build fortifications—that was the great protection for the French against the Germans. Yet, on this bright morning, German troops moved in, and that was an even clearer violation of the treaty. The French and British were obliged to attack. A German general said later that the whole of the Nazi regime would have fallen if only a few French troops had appeared, but they didn't. The Germans are just going into their garden. Neville Chamberlain and Stanley Baldwin were worried about the affects upon trade of any military action. So Hitler was given the power he needed—that the Allies would not respond. Openly, Stanley Baldwin and his closest associate, Neville Chamberlain, spoke of a policy of appeasement (that meant a policy of peace). Let's work things out, let's negotiate, and surely if Hitler is able to put troops into the Rhineland, that will satisfy him.

Churchill was already speaking out. He was being provided, at great risk, with confidential information about the size of the British military establishment, above all about its air force. He knew that in 1935, Stanley Baldwin, under constant questioning in Parliament from Churchill, had promised that the British air force would always be kept at parity, at the same level with the Germans. He knew the Germans had twice as many aircraft and so he kept questioning and probing. Finally the figures became too obvious for anyone to dispute, the Germans had far more planes. So he asked Stanley Baldwin and Baldwin's associates there in Parliament, how can you have promised to us that we would be kept in parity? And the Minister Defense Secretary Hoare said, well, the situation is fluid. Churchill said, "And so they go on, they go on decided to be undecided, resolute to be irresolute, adamant for drift, solid for fluidity, all-powerful to be impotent."

These are the years that the locust have eaten. The power of Germany was becoming too great to resist. Churchill began to build a following. An anti-Nazi league was formed. Leading members of Parliament and leading members of British life over all began to speak out against this Nazi danger, and once again the impetuosity of Churchill all but destroyed him. He had regained a considerable place of influence, and then, in the year 1936, Britain was shaken by a crisis that seems absurd to us looking back upon it. The old king had died and the new King Edward—debonair, playboy type, hated by Stanley Baldwin—became king. He had not married and one of the first tasks of an English sovereign is to produce children, heirs to the throne. Not only that, but he was openly keeping company with an American, a divorcée, a woman of loose standards, and a woman really too old to have children, Wallis Warfield Simpson. And he made it known that he was to marry her. The Prime Minister said, please talk with your mother about this. And the mother other said, you cannot marry her. He said, I love her, mom. And she said, I know, but she is utterly unsuited, she is divorced, that is against the Church of England. Well, maybe we can get that overseen. She can't have children. Well, maybe she can. She is an American. That is probably the worst thing about her I suppose, but what can we do? Stanley Baldwin said, sire, if you go ahead with this wedding, it will create a constitutional crisis, she cannot be queen, you must put her aside. Again his mother said, think about all the sacrifices the little people made during the last war, surely you can make this sacrifice. But Edward was determined and he found one champion—everybody else was opposed to it, the newspaper, the little people were opposed to it, they didn't want this American woman on the throne—one champion: Winston Churchill. Now his wife, Clementine, said, stay out of this, he is a silly little man, let him destroy himself. But no, Churchill asked permission of Stanley Baldwin, and goes and talks with the king. The king would later say when Mr. Baldwin spoke about the monarchy, it was a faint little thing, but Mr. Churchill infused it with vibrancy, it was a live thing, and I wanted to be king. So, he told Churchill, I will stay on, I will fight. But he didn't, he agreed to abdicate. But he didn't bother to tell Churchill he agreed to abdicate.

So Churchill goes into Parliament and starts to make a speech, I want the Prime Minister to promise that nothing final will be done… And there were shouts of anger, the visible hatred on the faces on the members of Parliament surpassed anything other members had ever seen. Sit down! Shut up! Churchill was astounded at this blast. He said, promise me that nothing final will be…and again he was drowned out. You won't be satisfied until you have broken him, he said to Baldwin, and the Dear Vicar, Baldwin, just sat there quietly. Churchill had destroyed himself and he wouldn't need to worry too much about more probing questions. The silly little man would

112          ©2001 The Teaching Company.

abdicate and go off to be a very silly little man with a silly little duchess over the years. Churchill's influence suffered a tremendous blow.

So step by step, first Hitler annexed Austria. Well, it was a German speaking country, let them have it. When Churchill's voice raised against this, it had little influence in Parliament. There were others outside Parliament who knew he was telling the truth, who knew how important it was to get his message. But even his best friend, Lord Beaverbrook, the great newspaper magnet, in this critical moment, stopped Churchill's column, would not have it printed. The BBC refused him the right to broadcast. And so would come then the great crisis at Munich. Neville Chamberlain, now Prime Minister, believing that Hitler kept his word—he was a man who could deal on a honest and honorable basis—would go off to Munich in September of 1938 and, with the French premiere, gave away Czechoslovakia, stripped of its northern frontier, allowed the Germans to occupy the northern part of Czechoslovakia and prepare the way for war. And such was the foolishness of people that when Neville Chamberlain came back and said, "I bring you peace in our time," they cheered. A few days later in Parliament, Churchill said:

> I do not deny our people the joy that they feel at the moment, but we have suffered a total unmitigated defeat. Silent, mournful, broken, abandoned, Czechoslovakia recedes into the darkness. She is suffered in every way by her association with the western democracies. Do not think that this is the end, it is but the beginning. It is a first taste of a bitter cup that will be proffered to us year by year unless, we recover by a supreme effort our moral strength and martial vigor and take out stand for freedom as in the olden times.

# Lecture Nine
# Rallying the Nation

**Scope:**

Churchill's prophecies proved true, and in 1939, Britain and France were found utterly unprepared for the total war waged by the seemingly invincible Nazi war machine. Leaders of the British government, including King George, thought the only hope for Britain lay in a negotiated peace with Germany. Such a desertion of the cause of freedom was unthinkable to Churchill. Assuming the prime ministership, Churchill felt that his whole past life "had been but a preparation for this hour and this trial." The fall of France marked the beginning of the Battle of Britain, 10 months of incessant bombing in which Hitler and his Luftwaffe sought to break the will of the British people. Our lecture follows Churchill as he leads the British in "their finest hour."

## Outline

I. The policies of Prime Minister Neville Chamberlain (1869–1940) had left Britain unprepared for war with Germany.

   A. In March 1939, Hitler broke promises he had made at the conference in Munich and seized the rest of Czechoslovakia.

   B. This blatant treachery finally began to shift the mood in Parliament.

   C. Churchill had urged an alliance with the Soviet Union, but Chamberlain rejected this idea and pushed Britain into an alliance with Poland.

   D. Stalin then turned where he could and made a fateful alliance with Hitler.

   E. This action opened the way for Hitler's invasion of Poland in September 1939.

   F. Britain and France declared war on Germany.

   G. Demands to bring Churchill back into the government grew, and Chamberlain made Churchill First Lord of the Admiralty.

**H.** In the meantime, Britain and France did nothing to defend Poland, which lost millions under Nazi tyranny in the years to come. Hitler was now convinced that Britain and France would not oppose him.

**II.** On April 9, 1940, the Germans opened their offensive with the invasion of Denmark and Norway. Barely two months later, on June 14, German troops were marching down the streets of Paris.

    **A.** The German offensive that began on May 10, 1940, against Belgium, the Netherlands, and France precipitated a crisis in the British government.

    **B.** Neville Chamberlain was forced to resign.

    **C.** There was deep pessimism at the very top of the British government.

        **1.** The Foreign Secretary, Lord Halifax, and King George VI were convinced that Britain could not win the war against Germany. David Lloyd George, who had been Prime Minister during World War I, believed the same thing. Other leading figures, such as the press baron Lord Beaverbrook, shared this view.

        **2.** They believed Britain must make a negotiated peace with Germany. Germany would dominate the continent of Europe. Britain would retain its Empire.

        **3.** Hitler was in favor of such a treaty.

    **D.** Churchill's record of warning against German aggression made him the obvious choice to become the new Prime Minister, but many leaders distrusted him.

    **E.** However, the canny Lord Halifax urged Churchill's appointment as Prime Minister. The idea was that Churchill would be forced to sign the peace treaty with Germany, be tarnished by this action, and be forced to step down. Then Halifax would become Prime Minister.

    **F.** Churchill accepted the challenge, and on May 10, 1940, became Prime Minister.

        **1.** He formed a coalition government, including representatives of all major parties, Labour, Liberal, and Conservative.

        **2.** Churchill also assumed the position of Minister for Defence. The combined offices of Prime Minister and

Minster for Defence enabled him to coordinate both the political and military efforts.

   **3.** He called for victory; anything less, he warned, would spell the end of the British Empire.

**III.** The surrender of the King of the Belgians left a large number of British and French troops cut off at Dunkirk.

   **A.** The evacuation of 336,000 French and British troops (May 26–June 3, 1940) bolstered British morale.

   **B.** Hitler's failure to send his armored forces to destroy the British and French troops was the first of those mistakes that would ultimately lose the war.

**IV.** The strategic disaster caused by the collapse of France was equaled by its impact on British morale.

   **A.** News of the imminent collapse of France shattered British morale.

   **B.** Lord Halifax insisted that Britain make a negotiated peace with Hitler; he wanted to give Mussolini strategic gains in the Mediterranean in return for Mussolini's intervention with Hitler on behalf of Britain.

   **C.** The Labour Party disagreed and backed Churchill.

   **D.** Churchill made it clear that he had no intention of negotiating peace.

   **E.** On June 4, 1940, Churchill delivered to Parliament his famous speech proclaiming, "We shall never surrender."

   **F.** Churchill would later modestly say that it was just his job to "give the roar to the British lion."

**V.** With the fall of France, the Battle of Britain began.

   **A.** From mid-June 1940 to mid-May 1941, the Germans bombed Britain in an effort to establish air superiority, break the will of the British people, and force a negotiated peace.

   **B.** The destruction was massive.

   **C.** Churchill watched the bombers coming in, refusing to stay in his bunker. Every day he walked the streets of London or visited other bombed cities, giving the "V" sign of victory and words of encouragement to the people who were suffering.

**D.** On August 16, during the heaviest onslaught up to that point of German aircraft attacks, Churchill was at fighter headquarters. Moved by the undaunted efforts and courage of the airforce, he uttered the legendary words: "Never before in the course of human conflict have so many owed so much to so few."

**Essential Reading:**

Gilbert, *Churchill*, pp. 623–700; *World War II*, pp. 1–138.

**Supplementary Reading:**

Berlin, *Churchill in 1940*.

Churchill, *Second World War*, volume II.

Hough and Richards, *Battle of Britain*.

Luckas, *Five Days in London*.

**Questions to Consider:**

1. Why do you think France surrendered and Britain fought on?

2. What does the Battle of Britain tell us about the effectiveness of strategic bombing?

# Lecture Nine—Transcript
## Rallying the Nation

In our last lecture, we saw storm clouds gather over Europe in the period from 1933 until 1939, when all the promise and hope that had accompanied the end of the First World War began to end in what would become an even more tragic and devastating struggle. We saw Britain led by Stanley Baldwin and Neville Chamberlain. Now these were not good, decent men trying to do the best they could in a difficult situation. They were politicians in the most odious sense of the word. Their concern was for their office and staying in that office. They could lie to a nation; they looked the British people in the eye and said we are militarily prepared. Their concern was for not loosing elections. Stanley Baldwin would say with absolute frankness that had he spoken frankly of the disparity between British strength and German strength, he would have lost the 1935 election. The extraordinary thing is Stanley Baldwin could not see anything bad in that statement; to him this was just politics. They were men who would be at home today in our political world.

If anything, Neville Chamberlain was worse than Stanley Baldwin—he had a self-righteous air to himself. He was from a distinguished political family. His father, Joseph, and his half brother, Austin, were politicians of great dimension in Britain. Neville was not raised to be a politician, he was going to be the business side of the family—he was a failure at it. But he went on to become Lord Mayor of Birmingham and rose to be Prime Minister through municipal government. That was always his attitude, the pinch-minded attitude of a bookkeeper and mayor. At the height of the controversy over King Edward and whether he should abdicate, rather than seeing this as a constitutional crisis, which it was for Churchill, here was a king being forced to abdicate without the matter ever having been discussed openly in Parliament, simply being forced to abdicate by the Prime Minister. This did not bother Neville Chamberlain at all, he was simply worried, as he told Baldwin, that this ongoing controversy might affect the Christmas trade. Let's get it settled as quickly as possible, so people will spend a lot for Christmas and not be worried. He was utterly incapable of understanding Hitler. He had no grasp of the dimensions of Hitler's mind and the dimensions of his grasp for power. But he also had the attitude that other people's freedom didn't matter: Czechoslovakia was a far away place, of

 ©2001 The Teaching Company.

which we knew little, so give it away. And, as Churchill said, "you think that you have sold honor and bought peace but you have sold honor and bought only war."

Indeed, in March 1939, Hitler would break every one of his promises made at the time of the Munich settlement in September of 1938 and seize what was left of Czechoslovakia. It was this blatant treachery that finally began to shift the mood in Parliament. In the course of that summer of 1939, now belatedly realizing that war was all but inevitable, Chamberlain blundered again. It was possible, as Churchill said over and over again during those months, to make an alliance with the Soviet Union. No one had spoken more harshly against communism than I have, said Churchill, but it is a question of priorities. We must make an alliance with the Soviet Union, that alone will check Hitler. But Chamberlain did not like the Bolsheviks. So, without making an alliance with the Soviet Union, that did push Britain into an alliance with Poland, and both France and Britain guaranteed Poland. So, Stalin turned where he could and make a fateful alliance with Adolph Hitler. This then opened the way for Hitler's invasion of Poland on September 1, 1939 and war was declared. Britain and France declared war upon Germany. So, barely 20 years after the end of the First World War in utter defeat of Germany, again, war.

The demand for Churchill to be included in the government had grown over the summer—newspapers and Parliament—it was demanded over and over again. Churchill must be part of the government. Chamberlain delayed as long as he could, and finally, on September 3, asked Winston Churchill to become, again, First Lord of the Admiralty (the position that he had lost in the wake of the Dardanelles catastrophe of 1915). Churchill came back to that office, and there was a secret cabinet that he opened up, and there were the maps, just as they had been left the last day he was in the Admiralty, all the ships. And he would write:

> Once again, after a quarter of a century, we face mortal danger at the hand of the same foe. Once again must Britain draw the sword in defense of a small nation outraged and invaded. Once again we must fight for life and honor against all the might and fury of the valiant disciplined and ruthless German race. Once again, so be it, so be it.

And he began to direct the Admiralty. Now, he had not been totally admired by all ranks in the navy. There were men in the navy who still remembered how, when he was meeting with chief admirals in 1915, and they told him, you are outraging the traditions of the navy. He said, "The traditions of the navy—sodomy and the lash—good day, gentlemen." But he was the man of the hour right now, and all over the British fleet, the signals flashed out: Winston is back. He began to take sure direction of the navy, even as he had done in 1914, when the first war broke out.

In the meantime, nothing much happened in terms of Britain and France fighting Germany. They sat still week after week, while their ally, Poland, was overrun. Now, France had the largest army in Europe—it was well equipped; it had a large air force—but it did nothing. The gallant Poles went down to defeat, to be enveloped in a dark period of servitude and viscous tyranny unsurpassed in the history of Europe. Millions of Poles died under the Nazi tyranny in the years to come. Their allies did nothing, only enhancing Hitler's belief that the Allies would, in fact, not fight. They had not fought at the Rhineland, they had not fought for Czechoslovakia (and France had a direct alliance with Czechoslovakia), and now they had not fought for Poland.

Then, the winter began to settle in over the front, what the newspapers would call the "phony war" or the Germans would call the *Sitzkrieg*. They had had the *Blitzkrieg*, the "lightning war" that swept over Poland, and now they had the *Sitzkrieg*, where they just sat. And while they prepared, and Hitler worked to the finest level his plan for the invasion of Western Europe, the French army's moral deteriorated. After all, the Soviet Union, the Communists were allies of the Germans and communist sympathies were strong among many Frenchmen, so the moral declined. Neville Chamberlain continued to believe that everything was okay, and on April 2, he made the most remarkable (in retrospect) statement to the Parliament, a statement which shows his complete lack of any grasp of what was going on. "Here Hitler," he said, "had missed the bus." He wasn't going to do anything, and he let his opportunity pass. Well, Churchill was one of several Cabinet members who were determined for action. The Allies should do something. So a small action was begun in Norway, in an effort to prevent Swedish iron ore from reaching the Germans. They needed that iron ore. Norway was neutral, Sweden was neutral, and the iron ore was coming down through Norway. So the British started a naval action with some landing of troops in April 1939. Then, suddenly, the Germans invaded Norway. They invaded Denmark, and in a matter of hours the Danes had capitulated, and Norway was under attack, and Oslo was occupied. Here Hitler has missed the bus—hardly!

The defeatism in Europe was such that the Danish king, surrendering after only a brief few shots had been fired by his guards, then said to the German general, "I surrender. And might I say, as an old soldier, it was a smartly carried out exercise." What an extraordinary statement. So, Denmark fell under the conquered nations. The Norwegians fought with bravery, but they could not resist, and the mood in Parliament became evermore angry. The situation in Norway was going to be the center of a strong debate in Parliament. As Chamberlain got up to begin his comments, the Parliament began to seethe with anger and words were heard like—go, go, go, go—he could barely complete his speech. And then the long-standing member of Parliament, Leo Amery, quoting Cromwell, and Cromwell had dismissed the Long Parliaments many years before: "You have sat too long [speaking to Chamberlain] for any good that you have done. Let us be done with you. In the name of God, go." As Chamberlain left the Parliament, there were those who feared for his physical safety as members of Parliament crowded around him, singing *Rule Britannia* and Go! Go! Go! Go!

Chamberlain was about to resign when suddenly, that May 10, Germans troops invaded Holland, Belgium, and France, and began to sweep through the Low Countries. That morning there was an extraordinary shock through out Britain. Churchill was awaken on the telephone to hear of this news and Chamberlain then said, well, maybe I had better stay on, it would be wrong to resign in the midst of this crisis, I'd better stay on, what I think I am going to do is form a national government, I want the Labour Party to join us. And he asked the head of the Labour Party, Clement Attlee, if Labour would be willing to serve in his government. Attlee said, I will have to check, and it is easy to check because we are having our annual convention at this moment, my suspicion, however, is they will serve under a Conservative Prime Minister, but not under you. And that was the answer: we will not serve under Chamberlain. So the question was, that fateful day, who will be Prime Minister? Churchill or Lord Halifax? Those were the two obvious candidates.

Lord Halifax was the Foreign Secretary, a distinguished man who had served as Viceroy of India, a solid proponent, solidly in favor of appeasement, appeasing Hitler. He was also another one of these men who was not decent. He was an anti-Semite and that played a significant role in his desire to appease Hitler. But he was the favorite of King George. He was a sound man, not impetuous like Churchill. And King George, like others, believed that Lord Halifax was the man to make a negotiated peace with the Germans, and that was all that was possible—to make that negotiated peace which would keep Britain's empire and let the Germans dominate the Continent. Churchill and Halifax spoke on that day, speaking together privately, and Halifax understood how delicate this situation was. His goal, as we mentioned in our first lecture, was to allow Churchill to become Prime Minister, allow Churchill to make the inevitable negotiated peace with the Germans, to be tarnished by it, to have to step down, and then Lord Halifax would become Prime Minister. So, he said to Churchill, I think it would be highly difficult for me to guide Parliament, and guide the Commons from the House of Lords (because he was a Lord and he sat in the House of Lords). Churchill did not say a word, for once in my life I was silent. Then Halifax said, I think you are probably the better man. Again, I said nothing.

So it would be Churchill who was called to King George that evening to be asked to accept the prime ministership. I don't suppose you can imagine why I called you here, said King George. No, I cannot your majesty. Then Churchill assumed this great burden. On May 13, he spoke to Parliament: "All I have to offer," he said, "is blood, toil, tears and sweat." "We," he said, "at this moment are faced with the greatest crisis in our long island history…You ask what is our policy?" Of course, that is what many minds are doing at a stage like this, running around, what is our policy, our aim?

> You ask what is our policy? It is to wage war. It is to wage war by sea, land, and air. It is to wage war with all our might and with all the strength that God can give us. It is to wage war against a monstrous tyranny unsurpassed in the lamentable catalogue of human crime … You ask what is our aim? I can answer in one word. It is victory. Victory despite all costs. Victory despite all terrors. Victory, no matter how long and hard the road may be, because without victory there is no survival. Let that be understood. Without

©2001 The Teaching Company.

victory there is no survival for the British Empire and all that empire has stood for.

So do you see? He has answered those who say we can make this negotiated peace—that would be to destroy what makes the empire special, can you grasp that? Why keep the empire—that is what Lord Halifax wants to do—if the law and liberty of the civilization that that empire represents vanishes? So it will, but the idea of a negotiated peace had not died. Hitler was quite convinced that Britain would make a negotiated peace.

Various reasons are given why Hitler, having driven the British and French to that narrow spit of land called Dunkirk after the Belgium king had surrendered, why Hitler did not send in his armor—he had plenty of tanks that could have crushed that army there on the beach—annihilated it—he did not. He was certainly persuaded in part by Herman Gering who wanted the glory of his air force, his Luftwaffe, winning the final stage of the battle. Hitler also had ideas that went back to the time of his own service in Flanders of how difficult that terrain was. But another crucial element was that this would be a kind of understanding with the British, that he had not utterly destroyed their army.

So, the evacuation of Dunkirk began, starting that May 27, hard and heavy fighting, Churchill thought he would have to bring out the tanks. The Luftwaffe was unable to stop that evacuation, that brave little fleet of royal naval vessels—of garbage scowls, of an American yacht—that ferried 336,000 British and French troops to safety. But at the very moment this evacuation was going, on May 28, there was a critical meeting of the Cabinet, two days before the French minister had come to London to say: we cannot hold out; we are collapsing and we will surrender; I see no other course. This Cabinet meeting was held to discuss what to do if, in fact, the French surrender. You have to understand the shock of this, the French army was thought to be the most powerful army in Europe and it was in utter ruin, how could this be? In 1914, they had fought on for four more years, and now it seemed as though within a matter of days the Germans would be marching down the streets of Paris. The reports that came back, both the official reports and private reports—Churchill had a close relative who was fighting in France and he brought back the report of the utter absence of fighting spirit among the French troops.

Churchill's own discussions among the French leaders show utterly shattered they were.

So, this was the situation. Churchill met with his Cabinet and Lord Halifax insisted upon a negotiated peace. We have already set up, through the foreign office, lines of communication with Mussolini. We will offer Mussolini significant strategic gains in the Mediterranean, almost certainly giving him the island of Malta (a key naval base of the British). In return, Mussolini—who is not yet in the war—will intercede with us and Hitler. He will arrange a conference, and we can make this negotiated peace, it is the only way, we cannot win. Well, most of the Conservative members were quite. Neville Chamberlain was still a member of the Cabinet (that is still another example of the magnanimous spirit of Churchill, he kept Chamberlain on). Neville Chamberlain said we must listen to this. Now, Lord Halifax spoke again very strongly, and the two members of the Cabinet who were most utterly opposed to this idea of an negotiated peace were the Labour members, above all Clement Attlee, and they backed Churchill to the hilt. Churchill said, I must ponder this, I would like to call a meeting of the entire Cabinet, not just the ones concerned with the war, but also all 25 ministers. They came in and Churchill spoke and said, "I will never make a peace with that man, you must understand that. No matter what happens in France, we will fight on. If the long history of our island nation is to end, let it end when each one of us lays choking blood on the ground." Suddenly members of Cabinet leaped up and ran around and began to pound him on the back. Nothing like it had ever been seen in the somber atmosphere of British politics. And he had it—he knew that Britain would fight on.

He would address Parliament on that fateful day, June 4, bringing news that 336,000 British and French troops and give those ringing words with which we opened our first lecture:

> Although large parts of Europe and many old and famous States had fallen or might fall into odious grasp of the Gestapo and the apparatus of Nazi rule, [he never pronounced "Nazi" the right way, remember he would not learn German, that beastly language, and he always called them "Nazzis"; to call them Nazis would be to give to much dignity to them] all the odious apparatus of Nazi rule, we shall not flag or fail. We shall go on to the end, we shall

©2001 The Teaching Company.

fight in France, we shall on the seas and on the oceans, we shall fight with growing strength and confidence in the air, we shall defend our island whatever the cost may be, we shall fight on the beaches, we shall fight on the landing grounds, we shall fight in the fields and in the streets, we shall fight in the hills; we shall never surrender.

So he spoke to the British people; so he spoke to Hitler, who thought there was going to be a negotiated peace; and so he spoke to America, to a Roosevelt who was hearing from his ambassador, Joseph Kennedy, that the British were not going to fight. So Churchill spoke. He had already spoken to the British people in this first broadcast as Prime Minister:

> I speak to you … in a solemn hour for our country, for our empire, for our allies, and for the whole world. You see this was no small local war, it was a war for the very soul of mankind…Behind us lie shattered nations and bludgeoned races: the Czechs, the Poles, the Norwegians, the Danes, the Dutch, the Belgians [and he would soon have to add the French], upon them will descend a night unbroken even by a star of hope unless we conquer, as conquer we must; as conquer we shall, we shall, we are going to win. Today is Trinity Sunday. Centuries ago words were written to be a call and a spur to the faithful servants of truth and justice: "Arm yourselves, and be ye men of valour, and be in readiness for the conflict; for it is better for us to parish in battle than to look upon the outrage of our nation and our alter. As the Will of God is in Heaven, so be it."

Ancient words rallying a people through one more great struggle. He would later say modestly, it was just my job to "give the roar to the British lion" and perhaps from time to time to show that lion where his claws might be set. But he was more than that, he was a leader who took a doubtful people (with every reason to believe they could not win) and make them rally and fight or die.

> What has been called the Battle of France [he said in June of 1940] is about to end. I expect the Battle of Britain is about to begin …itler knows that he must break us in this island if he is to win. This evil man, this repository of so many forms of soul destroying hatred, this embodiment of ancient wrongs and shames [what a description of Hitler] and he

thinks he is going to terrorize us by his bombings, what he is going to do is light a fire that will ultimately consume him until we, hand in hand with the New World, [already talking about the Americans going to have to get into this], will march to victory and rebuild the temple of man's freedom upon a foundation that can never be overthrown. This is a solemn hour, [he said], in the cause of freedom. That is what we are fighting for, not national aggrandizement, but for freedom for the individual rights of every man, woman and child in this world. We are not going to loose, and what we are fighting for is right.

So the bombing of Britain would begin in June and July, as Hitler laid plans for an invasion. It began with the shipping in the Channel, it then moved to the airfields of the RAF, and then finally, starting on September 7, 1940, to the indiscriminate bombing of London and other cities. Thousands of dead, massive destruction of cities, and unlike Hitler, who later on never visited a bombed city in Germany, he was too sensitive for it, Churchill watched the bombers coming in, refusing to stay in his bunker, and every day walked the streets of London, or visited the bombed cities, talking with the people who were suffering, holding up his sign, "V" for victory, and saying we can take it.

On August 16, the heaviest flight of German aircraft yet came over. Churchill was at fighter headquarters, he looked at the table and said, we have no more reserves, if the Germans send over another flight, it only takes six minutes to cross the Channel, what will we do? And his air marshal said, the men will just refuel and go up again. He got back into his car late that evening, his aide started to say something to Churchill, he simply put his hand on the man's shoulder and said: "Don't say a word, I am too moved. Never before in the course of human conflict have so many owed so much to so few."

    ©2001 The Teaching Company.

# Lecture Ten
# The Tide of War Turns

**Scope:**

In a war of powerful leaders, Roosevelt, Stalin, and Hitler, Churchill proved to be the supreme strategist. The Cabinet War Rooms in London still evoke the memory of Churchill as a wartime leader. Our lecture analyzes the skills that made Churchill so successful: his own military experience and personal courage, his creative power and innovative intellect, and his conviction of the justness of his cause. Unlike both Stalin and Hitler, he did not feel threatened by excellence, and he surrounded himself with men of superior ability and character. The Battle of the Atlantic, the German invasion of the Soviet Union, America's entry into the war, and the campaign in the Western Desert leading up to El Alamein were all tests of Churchill's abilities as a wartime leader.

# Outline

I.  Churchill rallied his countrymen with powerful rhetoric, which some have criticized as old-fashioned. But the concepts of valor, honor, and freedom that he spoke about never become old-fashioned. Churchill also understood how to use power, and he established an organization to conduct the war that was far superior to that of Hitler.

   A.  Hitler had a chaotic system, playing one party against another, making major decision without consulting his ministers. This was far from Churchill's method.

   B.  Churchill was Minister for Defence as well as Prime Minister. After October 1940, he was head of the Conservative Party and leader of the House of Commons.

   C.  Throughout the critical years of the war, he had the full support of the Parliament, resting on the support he enjoyed with the British public.

   D.  The three major parties agreed on an electoral truce for the duration of the war. The general election scheduled for 1940 was postponed and did not occur until 1945.

   E.  Churchill put in place a well-organized and efficient structure for waging the war.

1. His Cabinet was a coalition of members from all three parties, Conservative, Liberal, and Labour.
2. Churchill's deputy was the Labour Party leader Clement Attlee.
3. The War Cabinet was composed of some six to eight members, who concentrated on strategy and other questions related to directing the war effort. These included Cabinet members in charge of foreign affairs, budget, and labor.

II. In the summer of 1940, a German invasion of Britain seemed a very real possibility.

A. Hitler was planning just such an invasion—Operation Sea Lion.

B. Much of Britain's artillery had been left at Dunkirk.

C. From the outset, Churchill understood the significance of the absence of a German fleet.

D. He also knew he had to stop the German airforce.

E. The British were aided all through the war by Ultra—the decoding of the German ciphers.

F. The origins of Ultra lay with Polish mathematicians, who passed their knowledge on to the French and British. By the summer of 1940, the British were reading German codes.

G. Thus, the British were able to determine that the German planes were sighting British targets by means of radio beams and were able to jam the beams.

H. They also learned about Hitler's invasion plans and his naval strength.

I. In the same way, they later learned that he had changed his plan and was focusing on Russia.

III. In the summer and fall of 1940 and throughout 1941–1942, Britain had to focus as well on Egypt and the danger that the pro-German Italians would try to capture the Suez Canal.

A. The knowledge that Hitler had called off his plan to invade Britain, gained through Ultra, was crucial to Churchill's decision to send reinforcements to Egypt.

©2001 The Teaching Company.

**B.** Churchill found an outstanding general in Bernard Montgomery, who defeated General Erwin Rommel and the Afrika Korps at El Alamein in the fall of 1942.

**IV.** In 1940, Churchill's role as war leader also focused on bringing the United States into the war as the only possible salvation for Britain.

   **A.** Churchill carefully developed ties with President Franklin Roosevelt that, in 1940–1941, made the United States into a military partner of Britain and made it possible for Roosevelt to direct the major effort of the United States against Germany, rather than Japan.

   **B.** Similarities in background and experience enhanced the personal relationship between Churchill and Roosevelt, "the best friend Britain ever had."

   **C.** Hundreds of letters passed between the two men.

   **D.** The United States was reluctant to get into the war, remembering all its debtors from World War I, including Britain, which owed the United States a great deal of money.

   **E.** Churchill, however, was determined to obtain aid from the United States, even turning over British accounts to American inspection.

   **F.** He finally succeeded, and in the spring of 1941, the American lend-lease program began, which would finance the much-needed development of British military equipment.

**V.** On December 7, 1941, the Japanese attacked Pearl Harbor. Three days later, Hitler declared war on the United States.

   **A.** Hitler's gratuitous declaration of war against the United States on December 10, 1941, was a mistake as serious as his invasion of the Soviet Union.

   **B.** With America's entry into the war, Churchill could believe that ultimate victory was certain.

**VI.** The German invasion of the Soviet Union, Germany's former ally, began on June 22, 1941. It was a mistake from which Hitler never recovered.

   **A.** Making use of Ultra, Churchill had warned Stalin of Hitler's intentions.

**B.** Despite his long opposition to communism, Churchill turned with intelligent alacrity to supporting the Soviet Union in every way possible in its struggle with Germany.

**VII.** The Americans, under General Marshall, wanted to attack the Germans directly in Europe. Churchill was dubious of a quick success in "fortress" Europe.

**A.** As in World War I, Churchill was a proponent of peripheral campaigns.

**B.** North Africa presented the one area in which a successful campaign against the Axis powers was possible for the British.

**C.** The Americans argued strongly against it; Marshall thought Churchill's plan was redolent of the Dardanelles.

**D.** But on November 8, 1942, Operation Torch began in Morocco and Algeria.

**E.** The North African campaign was a major tactical and strategic success.

**F.** The German and Italian forces were caught between the Allied army in the west and the British army under Montgomery in the east.

**G.** The victory at El Alamein coincided with the Allied landings.

**H.** The Axis armies in North Africa were annihilated. By May 13, 1943, more than 250,000 troops had surrendered. The Allies suffered 76,000 casualties.

**VIII.** At the Casablanca Conference from January 14–24, 1943, Churchill won over the Americans to his plan for an invasion of Sicily to follow the North African campaign.

**A.** On August 16, the American forces entered Messina and the conquest of Sicily was complete.

**B.** The Allied invasion of Sicily led, on July 25, 1943, to Mussolini's fall from power and kept German troops tied down in Italy.

**C.** This was Britain's high point of strategic influence in the war.

 ©2001 The Teaching Company.

**IX.** The ever-growing might of the United States, the fact that Britain had become a debtor nation to the United States, and the growing strength of the Soviet Union all reduced Britain to a third partner in the alliance.

    **A.** Churchill believed, as Marlborough had, in personal diplomacy. In the course of the war, he made trip after trip to talk with Allied leaders.

    **B.** By the end of 1944, Churchill began to think that the defeat of Germany could bring forth an even greater threat of tyranny—from the Soviet Union.

    **C.** At Yalta, with Roosevelt and Stalin, he little knew that, in a few months, all his power and offices would be stripped from him.

## Essential Reading:

Gilbert, *Churchill*, volume VII: *Road to Victory; World War II*, pp. 138–365.

Gooch, "Churchill as War Leader," in Dear, *Oxford Companion to the Second World War*, pp. 235–242.

## Supplementary Reading:

Hamilton, *Monty*.

Lamb, *Churchill as War Leader*.

Lewin, *Churchill as Warlord*.

## Questions to Consider:

**1.** Do you agree that Churchill's vast experience in naval matters was a critical factor in his success as a wartime leader?

**2.** Why do you think Hitler invaded the Soviet Union? Was it the decisive event in World War II?

# Lecture Ten—Transcript
## The Tide of War Turns

As so war came to Europe. In our last lecture, we saw that on May 10, 1940, Churchill became Prime Minister amidst what some called "the darkest days in the history of England"—what Churchill would call "the sternest days in the long history of our island race." He rallied his countrymen—"Be Ye Men of Valor"—we are fighting to restore the temple of man's freedom and honor. Valor, freedom, honor: old-fashioned words some thought, even at the time. In critiquing Churchill today, historians will tell you that his rhetoric belonged to what they really wrongly called the Antonine Age of British rhetoric"—old-fashioned, florid. I would say they are dead wrong. Honor, valor, freedom: these words never become old-fashioned. They are eternal truths. They are as enduring at this moment as they had been throughout history. That is what Churchill's audience understood. He spoke to an audience that deep in their hearts believed in truth and justice, honor and freedom—that these were noble things worth fighting for and dying for. Hitler would have said no. He lied and he took words like honor and truth and perverted them. "Our Honor is Loyalty" was the slogan of the SS, but a complete perversion of a noble idea.

Churchill, however, also understood and he said, "You do not win wars by rhetoric." If Britain were to survive, and ultimately to triumph, he had to use his power as Prime Minister, and he knew how to use power. We can visit today the Cabinet War Rooms in the heart of London. They are, at this moment, the way they were at the end of the war in Europe. We can feel the presence of Churchill there in that underground bunker, provided with all the facilities to conduct the war. We can witness as he formed his coalition Cabinet—it will be a war fought by a national government—he will include Labour, what remains of the Liberal Party, and his deputy Prime Minister will be Clement Attlee as head of the Labour Party. They will function and work together, not only to win the war, but also increasingly to build a blue print for a new Britain that will emerge from the war. He has core of six to eight men who form the War Cabinet—including the Minister for Labor and the Minister for Foreign Secretary—he establishes a smooth functioning general staff to serve as his liaison forces and to put his policies into affect and to advise him. Unlike Hitler, he does not think he is the supreme general. In fact, he would say perhaps the greatest single ally we had in the war, next to the Americans, was Corporal Schickelgruber and his strategic brilliance. (Schickelgruber, of course, being a name that had been used by Hitler's grandfather at one point.) Corporal Schickelgruber and his strategic brilliance perhaps did more than anything else to win the war for us.

Well, Churchill, in fact, has a strategic sense, but he allows himself to be guided by his generals and by his admirals. We see him there in the Cabinet War Rooms, dashing around in his boiler suit or siren suit, as he called it. It zipped up the front, got into it like a jump suit and zipped it up, he had a variety of them. One of them was green velvet, one was purple velvet, but for more formal occasions he had pin striped one; he would wear that with his bow tie. There were various reasons for having that suit, but Churchill and I both know why, so you don't have to keep pulling up your pants all the time. You have that on and you can concentrate on what is going on rather than the possibility that your pants are going to fall down. At 5'6" and 215 pounds, this enormous waist, and of course, he continued to eat during the war. He had an amazing memory for food, you can picture how much he liked to eat. When he was writing about the moments right before the attack of Omdurman. He describes how they stopped for lunch, laid out plates of bully beef and mixed pickles. He also described the lunch he had when he flew to France to buck up the French—their armies were collapsing in 1940—the soup, and a cold chicken, and the white wine that they had. One of his memos issued during the war was, I guess there was a desire to lower the meat ration of the ordinary British workers, and he said, "I can imagine nothing that would depress the British worker more than having his meat ration cut, give them good red beef. Most of the world's problems are caused by food famines, potato eaters, vegetarians, non-smokers, and teetotalers. I have it on good authority that Adolph Hitler is a vegetarian, he is a complete teetotaler, he abhors smoking, I rest my case."

But it took more than jocular memos to win this war. Churchill understood that the first step was for Britain to survive. In the summer of 1940, the idea of a German invasion of Britain loomed very real—an invasion by sea, accompanied by heavy destruction from the air—and Hitler was planning just such an invasion: Operation Sea Lion. Much of the equipment of the British army had been left in France at Dunkirk. At one point the only fully equipped division in Britain was the Canadian division. How would you stop such an invasion? From the outset Churchill understood the absence of a German fleet and the significant role that would play in this kind of invasion. Then, you had to stop the Luftwaffe, and that, as we saw in our last lecture, was done during the Battle of Britain.

But key to it all was knowing the German plans, and here the British were aided all through the war, as we Americans would be, by Ultra. That is the coding of the German ciphers. This had already begun in Poland by Polish mathematicians. The knowledge had been passed onto the French and to the British, and already, by the summer of 1940, the British were reading German codes. They would do so with varying success all through the war, and that was key. It had to be done in just such a way that the Germans never understood that the British had their code. By reading that code the British learned how the German planes were sighting in on British target air fields, how they were coming in on radio beams, and once they knew that, they could jam those beams, throwing the Germans off target. They could also read the struggles that were going on among Hitler's leaders, his military men and his admirals, over whether an invasion was possible, how many ships could be found, how every kind of tugboat and barge and the like was being mustered for an invasion. Then, they could see the effect that the Battle of Britain was having; judging that they were taking down at least two, maybe three times as many German aircraft as for every British aircraft that was lost. Then, gradually seeing Hitler giving up hope for an invasion. By October of 1940, it was clear from these codes that Hitler was dismantling his plans for an invasion of Britain—what a key set of knowledge that was—and instead he was looking eastward to invade Russia. So survival lay first in wining the Battle of Britain.

But there was another way that Britain could be knocked out of the war, in which Churchill's government would almost certainly fall, a negotiated peace would be essential for the British, and that was to capture the Suez Canal. To capture the Suez Canal, to drive Britain out of Egypt, to sever the line from Britain to India: that was very possible in the summer and fall of 1940 and into the spring of 1941. British rule was hated in Egypt; there were strong nationalist forces demanding the overthrow of the British, and there was Germany's ally, Italy, ruling Libya. In the summer of 1940, barely into the war, the Italians began their offensive against the very meager British forces holding Egypt. That was another major strategic demand:

How much could be sent to Egypt? How much could be sent from Britain to Egypt? Again, knowing the German code, knowing the declining likelihood of a British invasion by the Germans, Churchill made the decision to send reinforcements to Egypt. So would begin the long seesaw battle in the western desert.

On February 12, 1941, the most brilliant of German generals, Erwin Rommel, distinguished for bravery in the First World War, master of tank warfare, brilliant in the campaign in France, now took charge of the German and Italian forces, creating his famed Afrika Korps. It would be a campaign fought with chivalry. No SS divisions were there, and Churchill would speak openly of his admiration for Rommel. He would come so close to capturing Cairo, but it never quite happened. There in the western desert, in 1942, Churchill would discover his General Bernard Montgomery, and in the climatic battle at El Alamein, starting on October 22 and 23 with a huge artillery bombardment, the Afrika Korps would be broken and the tide of war would begin to turn. So the risk in the desert paid off. Privately Churchill would say of Montgomery: "indomitable in retreat, invincible in advance, and insufferable in victory." But to those Tommy's who fought there, he would say at the great amphitheater at Carthage as he addressed them, that "the brave men who turned the tide of war in the western desert, like their comrades in the skies above Britain, will deserve the gratitude, the admiration, and the reverence of this island nation for as long as we endure as a people."

Just a personal note, I was traveling with Mrs. Fears in Scotland, and there was a castle that had been turned into a bed and breakfast. It was castle of an ancient family. When you walked in you saw the suits of armor, and you saw the pictures on the walls of the family members who had served as officers in the Crimea and Omdurman. We were told by the manager of the castle that the last of the line had died at El Alamein in the final breakthrough by the 51st Highland Division. We were sitting there in some silence and this little lady who was also one of the guests piped up, "My husband was in El Alamein, he was decorated for bravery." So I looked around the room for some giant heroic figure, there was this little bitty man, a postman, and he said simply, "War is just a matter of luck." But you see, Churchill understood that is who fought and won these wars, these ordinary British Tommy's, men who wanted nothing so much as to get back to their homes, but he could inspire them.

Now, there was another key element in winning this war. At the very height of the bombing of London, during the blitz, Randolph, Churchill's son, was there with his father, and Churchill was shaving, and Randolph said, what are we going to do, Papa? Churchill said, I will drag America into this. And that was his goal from the start, to get America involved. There in the Cabinet War Rooms there is a little cabinet that says "Restroom for Prime Minister's use only." Well, in fact, it was a telephone room where Churchill could speak directly to President Roosevelt. They had met briefly at the end of the First World War in France, and Roosevelt wrote to Churchill, already in September of 1939, "We are both former naval personnel, you are back in office and I am delighted to see it. If from time to time you would like to keep me informed about the progress of events, I would be most obliged." Churchill got the permission from then still Prime Minister Chamberlain and they began their correspondence. Hundreds and hundreds of letters in the course of the war between Winston Churchill, the great admirer of the United States, and Franklin Roosevelt, "the best friend Britain ever had." Churchill spared no facts from the president—we are going to loose unless you give us aid, and if we loose do you really think the Germans will not attack you?

Roosevelt was strongly devoted to the cause of freedom, but it was not easy to give Britain aid before the United States went into the war. There was a strong isolationist movement in this country. Many members of our Congress did not want to get involved in Europe— we did it before, didn't we? And we got nothing out of it except a lot of unpaid debts. In the First World War, the only country that paid its debts back to us was Finland, and Britain was one of the largest debtors to us. There was legislation in place that said unless a country had paid back its WWI debts it would not get any aid. Churchill was not only determined to get aid—and Roosevelt, a very cunning man, knew this—but to get America so tangled up in it that America would have to come into the war. So, step-by-step they proceeded, Roosevelt being a very hard bargainer. If we are going to give you worn out destroyers, battleships, you have got to give us naval bases. Well, the British gave us naval bases in the Bahamas and elsewhere. They finally ended up with nine warships out of that deal, not the fifty, hard bargaining. We don't have any more money, Mr. President, Churchill said. Let's see your books, you got to turn over all your books. Well, why not? And Churchill did, as a statement of his tremendous faith and confidence. Roosevelt, a man of considerable wealth, looked through there and said there is lots of money there, and so, more demands for payment.

But he was determined to help Britain. He made use of little metaphors, similes: what if your neighbor's house were on fire, and your neighbor ran and said, "Give me a garden hose to put it out." Wouldn't that be easier than letting your own home catch on fire. And if the garden hose got a little damaged would you be that upset? So began, starting it the spring of 1941, the great lend-lease program by which we gave aid to Britain, ultimately to the Soviet Union, a total of 50 billion dollars—the money, the ships, the munitions that kept Britain fighting that were used there in the western desert.

Until, finally, on December 7, 1941, the Japanese would attack Pearl Harbor. Then three days later, Corporal Schickelgruber would make another one of his brilliant strategic decisions, to declare war upon the United States. Now, we had not declared war on Germany; Japan had attacked us. Congress and the mood of the country would have been: Fight the Japanese, they are the bad ones. But without even consulting his generals, Hitler declared war upon the United States. If you have ever seen the scene in the newsreels, his general's mouths literally drop open as he is declaring war, and this is all Roosevelt needs. Now a major American effort can be devoted against this treacherous, evil man who so unnecessarily declared war upon us. So, America is in it, and Churchill said, I knew then the war was won.

But another tremendous strategic mistake by Hitler had already begun to turn the tide, and that was on June 22, convinced that he could not take Britain, he launched his invasion of his ally, the Soviet Union. All along a huge front on that 22$^{nd}$ of June in 1941 the huge barrage began, and the invincible German army rolled into the land of the Soviets. Now, at the very moment that German troops were invading, Stalin's trains were bringing supplies to Germany. He was fulfilling every part of the treaty, despite constant warnings of the massing of German troops. Stalin refused to believe that this was going to happen. Making use of Ultra, of the decipherment of the German codes, Churchill told Stalin, this is going to happen and you are going to be invaded, and the invasion came. The question would be: What would this life long opponent of Bolshevism do? How would Churchill respond to this? And asked privately on the day before he was to give his speech to Parliament, he said, "If Hitler invaded hell I would make a favorable reference to the devil in the House of Parliament." And instead he spoke and said, "I take back not a word I have said about communism over the years. But who our ally is is the one who is fighting against Hitler. We will give all possible aid to the Soviet Union." And he did, taking weapons that Britain needed to ship to the Soviet Union.

Another critical strategic area was the Atlantic itself—to keep the supplies going between Britain and America—and the war of the Atlantic was greatly aided again by the Ultra, and by Churchill's experience of the First World War and how to deal with the great submarine menace. The Germans had very little of a fleet, the most powerful ship, the *Bismarck*, was knocked out of the war. But the submarines were a great threat; in various months, large amounts of shipping were lost—but it kept on and on—so, too, from Britain to the Soviet Union through the Arctic waters. In one particular month, 23 ships out of 30 were sunk, but the aid went on and on. That same December 1941, when the Japanese attacked Pearl Harbor, the Germans were right at the gates of Moscow, and Stalin unleashed his huge winter offensive with crack troops brought from Siberia, and the Germans never again would reach Moscow.

So, the tide of war was turning, and it moved now into the arena of a grand alliance, the kind of alliance that Marlborough had (referring to the first lecture). The Soviet Union, the United States, and Britain waging this war. Churchill had a clear idea of what the strategy should be. When the Americans came into the war, it was the goal of the Americans, of General Marshal and his staff, to get into Europe as quickly as possible; that was how you would win the war, by invading France and defeating the German army there. Churchill was dubious, it would take at least two years for the American manpower and equipment to be capable of attacking the fortress that was Europe. He wanted a peripheral attack, for the Allies to land in North Africa, to trap the German and Italian forces between the British army in the east and the Allies coming from the west. The first thought that the Allied commanders had, that Marshal had, was the Dardanelles all over again. Will he never get these amphibious operations out of his mind? They argued strongly against it. Churchill argued just as strongly for it, until it was launched on November 8, 1942, Operation Torch.

The Battle of El Alamein had been won four days before, and Churchill was asked: Can't we ring the church bells in England now, they have been silent since the beginning of the war? He said, let us wait. Then, as the Allied landing succeeded, in mid-November the bells began to ring out all over England once again, sounding out victory. Sure enough, by the spring of that year, 1943, trapped between the triumphant British forces under Montgomery and the American forces in which General Patton came to the fore, George Patton, our greatest fighting general, the Germans and Italians would undergo a defeat and a loss of men in terms of dead and prisoners equal to that lost at Stalingrad. It was a tremendous victory.

Then, Churchill pressed on for another peripheral action. Instead of just continuing to prepare to invade France, he wanted to invade Sicily. Italy was still very much an ally of the Germans; Mussolini very much still in power. Again, he had to fight it through a most reluctant American command. It was at Casablanca, in January of 1943 that he met with President Roosevelt, one of several meetings he would have with Roosevelt. There he convinced the Americans to undertake the invasion of Sicily, and on July 10 it would happen. And the Americans army came of age fighting in Sicily—"Born at sea, baptized in blood"—as one of its proudest divisions would say. Within a month and a half, Sicily had fallen, Generals Montgomery and Patton had marched into Messina, Mussolini had fallen from power, and Italy would join the Allied side. Now, it was a tremendous blow to the Germans. They would not give up Italy. But it was a grand Allied success that would keep dozens of German divisions tied down in Italy.

That was the high point of Churchill and his influence and strategy during the war. The ever growing might of America, putting two and three men into the field for every one that the British could, the fact that Britain had become a debtor nation to the United States, and the growing might of the Soviet Union, all reduced Britain to the third partner in this grand alliance. Churchill believed, as Marlborough did, in personal diplomacy, and in the course of the war, he would make trip after trip to Washington, to Stalin, on his own, as well as to the great conferences at Teheran, and Yalta, and Potsdam. After having flown from London to Cairo, reviewing the British troops there, and then flying up to meet with Stalin, to explain to him why there would be no new front in France opening that year, why the British had to cut back on their convoys through the Arctic, because of losses, dealing with a very angry Stalin, who said, you are just afraid to fight the Germans, sooner or later you British are going to have fight them. Churchill said, as man and a soldier, I would take the greatest exception, except for the bravery with which your men are fighting, Stalin said, you are probably right. Churchill said, I knew they understood only one thing—strength—and you must negotiate from strength.

When he got back from that trip, Douglas MacArthur, our general in the Pacific Theater, sent a memo to Churchill saying, "If you would just give me command of British decorations for one day, I would award you the Victoria Cross...It is the duty of a young pilot to fly thousands and thousands of miles, but for a man like you, with all your responsibilities, it is an act of heroism." And so it was. By the end of 1944, in the beginning of 1945, Churchill began to think back upon history. As the defeat of Spain, at the time the Spanish Armada, brought forth France as the new dominate power on the Continent and the threat to freedom, as the defeat of France during the Napoleonic wars brought to the fore Prussia, then Germany as the new threat. Would not this defeat of Germany bring forth an even greater threat? In a tyranny every bit as blood stained as that of the Nazi's, the Soviet Union. Now the time was to think beyond a wartime alliance and to whether Europe, after all this carnage, would indeed march into the bright uplands of freedom. Churchill, the statesman, he pondered these problems as he met with the dying Roosevelt and a triumphant Stalin at Yalta. He little knew that within a few months all of his power and offices would be stripped from him by the British electorate.

©2001 The Teaching Company.

# Lecture Eleven
# Champion of Freedom

**Scope:**

Churchill was determined that the victory of freedom in World War II should not be squandered as it had been after World War I. Throughout his political life, Churchill despised socialism and communism, resting as they do on the denial of one of the most basic of human rights: the right to property. Believing as he did in absolute right and wrong, Churchill though it wrong to replace the tyranny of Hitler with the tyranny of Stalin in central Europe. At home, he sought to convince the British people of the dichotomy between socialism and their tradition of liberty. In the moment of victory in 1945, the British people chose not to elect Churchill. At the age of 70, Churchill found himself again in the political wilderness, as Britain went down the road of socialism and began to dismantle its Empire. In his speech in Fulton, Missouri, in 1946, Churchill warned of an "Iron Curtain" falling across Eastern Europe. Like much else in his life, Churchill's speech was controversial. However, like much else as well, it was prophetic. The expansionistic policies of the Soviet Union led to his reelection as Prime Minister in 1951. For four years, he worked to establish the closest possible ties between Britain and the United States, the two great bastions of freedom. His last nine years saw him decline in health but never in his commitment to the principles he lived. As he told the boys of Harrow, his old school, "Never give up, never, never, never."

## Outline

**I.** Of the key figures of World War II, none had the military experience of Churchill, who also had a greater knowledge of history. Too, Churchill had a sense of foresight that was not shared by the other leaders.

    **A.** He became increasingly worried in 1943 and 1944 that the follies of World War I would be repeated.

    **B.** He was skeptical of the planned Normandy invasion because of his horror of massive loss of life.

**C.** The powerful fortifications that the Germans had erected along the French coast reminded Churchill of the casualties incurred by the British and French by such frontal assaults in World War I.

**D.** As he wrote, history can be an impediment, as well as an aid, to making decisions in the present.

**E.** He believed that man was unteachable, although he himself sought to teach, as he tried to warn Roosevelt against Stalin and the Soviets.

**F.** When the decision to invade Normandy was made, however, Churchill gave the operation his full support.

**II.** At Yalta in 1945, Churchill understood clearly that he was the junior partner in the coalition.

   **A.** Decisions were discussed by Stalin and Roosevelt as though he were not present. Although they had helped develop the atomic bomb, the British were not consulted when the Americans dropped the bomb.

   **B.** At Yalta, Churchill tried to make Roosevelt understand the danger represented by the Soviet Union.

   **C.** Roosevelt and the Americans were unwilling to challenge the Russian takeover of Poland. Churchill fought unsuccessfully to have the exiled Polish government play a role in post-war Poland, and Britain did not have the power to enforce his wishes.

**III.** In the midst of the Potsdam Conference, in July 1945, Churchill lost the British general election and ceased to be Prime Minister.

   **A.** In May 1945, the Labour Party held its annual convention and announced that it wanted an election. Churchill agreed.

   **B.** The war with Japan was still raging when the elections were called.

   **1.** No general election had been held during the war, and the Labour Party was insistent on holding an election as soon as possible.

   **2.** The election was held on July 5, 1945.

   **C.** Under the British system, the voters do not directly elect the Prime Minister. They elect the members of Parliament. The party that wins the largest number of seats in Parliament then chooses the Prime Minister.

    **D.** The British voters wanted a change: "Cheer for Churchill, vote for Labour" was the slogan of the day.

        **1.** The Conservative Party was still discredited by the bungling policies of Neville Chamberlain that had led Britain into the war.

        **2.** The voters wanted the broad program of social and economic reform associated with the socialism of the Labour Party.

        **3.** Churchill ran a poor campaign, largely a negative attack on socialism.

        **4.** Churchill had strong opposition from the labor unions.

        **5.** Many ordinary British voters disliked Churchill for what they saw as his anti-labor stance and other past mistakes. For many, his support during the war rested on the belief that he alone was strong enough and determined enough to see Britain through the crisis. But, as the voters saw it, the war was now over.

    **E.** The result, announced on July 26, was a landslide. That same day, Churchill resigned.

    **F.** It was a crushing blow to Churchill. Ironically, there was much in the Labour plan of which he approved.

**IV.** From 1945 to 1951, Churchill remained in Parliament.

    **A.** He worked on his history, *The Second World War*, in effect, his memoirs.

    **B.** He painted.

    **C.** He brooded over the dangers of the atomic bomb.

    **D.** He sought to warn the free world of the Soviet menace.

    **E.** His Iron Curtain speech at Fulton, Missouri, in March 1946 expressed this warning in its most dramatic form.

        **1.** As in the 1930s, many political leaders and the press attacked him for his alarmist and warmongering views.

        **2.** President Truman disavowed the speech.

    **F.** In 1947, at the University of Zurich, he gave a speech proposing a United States of Europe, all of which would work together for harmony and peace. It would take more than 50 years for his vision to work out. Already in his speech at Fulton, Missouri, he had asked Americans to form a fraternal alliance with Britain.

**V.** Growing concerns over Soviet expansion and worries about a third world war led to a change in the British voters. In 1951, the Conservative Party won a slight majority, and Churchill returned to serve as Prime Minister from 1951–1955.

> **A.** As Prime Minster for a second time, Churchill worked for European unity and for closer ties with the United States.
>
> **B.** But he understood that although Britain and the United States might have the same ideals, they did not share all the same interests.
>
> **C.** President Dwight Eisenhower and his administration were opposed to the continuation of the British Empire.
>
> **D.** In fact, the British Empire was coming to an end.
>
> **E.** Churchill feared that bloodshed on a large scale would be the result of granting India her independence; he believed that the British Empire was a moral force.
>
> **F.** But when India's independence became a reality, Churchill offered to do everything he could to help it.
>
> **G.** He wanted Britain to use its moral authority for détente between the Soviet Union and the United States, and after Stalin's death, he worked tirelessly to convince President Eisenhower to begin the process of détente. But it never came about.
>
> **H.** Churchill stepped down on April 5, 1955. His last words to his ministers were "never be separated from the Americans."

## Essential Reading:

Cannadine, *Speeches of Churchill*, pp. 269–314.

Gilbert, *Churchill*, pp. 844–959.

## Supplementary Reading:

Carlton, *Churchill and the Soviet Union*.

Charmley, *Churchill*, pp. 453-649.

Muller, *Churchill's Iron Curtain Speech*.

Young, *Churchill's Last Campaign*.

 ©2001 The Teaching Company.

**Questions to Consider:**

1. Would you have voted for Churchill in 1945?
2. Did Churchill exaggerate the Soviet menace?

# Lecture Eleven—Transcript
## Champion of Freedom

In our last lecture, we discussed Churchill as a wartime leader. His was an age of titanic figures: Stalin, Hitler, and Roosevelt. In terms of comparing these four great figures, Churchill certainly brought to his role as wartime leader an experience that none of them had—he had been a soldier in battle, as in fact, Hitler had been. But Churchill had led troops at a high level, as Lieutenant Colonel of the 6th Royal Scots Fusiliers. But he had also had command at the Cabinet level during the First World War—First Lord of Admiralty. None of these leaders could match that: Stalin himself had almost no military career, playing a little bit of a role during the Russian Civil War; Hitler certainly never having commanded at that kind of level, until he became Chancellor; and Roosevelt was not a military man, he had had a fairly minor office during the First World War, Undersecretary of the Navy. Churchill also brought a historical knowledge that none of them had: Stalin was in no sense of the word a scholar; neither was Hitler; Roosevelt read some history for pleasure. Churchill was a serious historian who had written about the lessons of history. His study of John, the Duke of Marlborough, his great ancestor, was a study in how to lead a grand alliance.

Churchill also had a sense of foresight that none of these other leaders had. For it is the chief quality of a statesman, it is the most important part of a statesman, having a vision. Remember our first lecture, we defined a statesman as one who has a bedrock of principles, a moral compass, a vision, and the ability to build a consensus to achieve that vision. Well, foresight is critical to having a vision. It is the ability to look into the future, to recognize problems and to come up with solutions that are good for both the short and the long term. What so troubled Churchill at the end of the First World War, and increasingly in 1943 and 1944, was the grave worry that the same follies would be repeated: how the Western powers at the end of the First World War threw away all of their advantages and plunged the world into another such carnage.

Surely, we must learn from the past, though Churchill was dubious of this. "From the cradle to the grave, man is unteachable," he said; he said that early in his life and late in his life. But he sought to teach, and he sought to teach Roosevelt about the danger represented by the Soviet Union and by Stalin. "History," Churchill wrote, "can be an impediment as well as an aid to action in the present."

He openly admitted that he had been highly skeptical of the Normandy invasion. He had tried to put it off as long as he could, because I had before me the vision of those great frontal assaults of World War I and the enormous loss of manpower. North Africa, Sicily, these were nothing compared to the invasion of France with the massive fortifications that had been laid down by the Germans, particularly under Rommel. But the invasion was planned and ready to go, and as you will recall, the weather was extremely bad. Eisenhower had to make the choice whether to send his men over and risk an utter rout as a result of the weather or to hold off and let the Germans get evermore prepared; let them perhaps discover that the assault was going to come in Normandy and not at Calais. Churchill was with Eisenhower when that decision was being made, and when it was done, having inspected Americans troops, having shaken the hands of paratroopers who would die that next day in France, Churchill said to Eisenhower, General, I am with you in this until the end. Eisenhower would later say, I knew he meant it, he was a leader who took responsibility and would not leave me hanging out there.

Years later Eisenhower would give an interview about Churchill as a military man with Alistair Cooke, the famous British and American journalist. Eisenhower said, he had a very keen strategic sense, don't let anybody tell you he was amateur. The interviewer said, well, didn't he do very badly in school? And Eisenhower said, if you ever studied my record at West Point, it wasn't very good either. But Churchill did well at Sandhurst, Eisenhower pointed out, and when I went to the Staff College, a far more rigorous place than West Point, I passed out first. People mature differently, and the man I knew was a strategic mastermind. He played a very important role in developing strategies, so this from a very good source.

So, the war would be won. Churchill would follow the Americans paratroopers, stand and salute their graves in Luxembourg and Belgium. He would stop, and just like General Patton, piss in the Rhine. The Germans had brought this all on. It had been so unnecessary. Then, as the war was winding down, at Yalta in 1945, he understood clearly that he was the junior partner in the coalition; decisions were discussed by Stalin as though he were almost not present at times. Typical was the fact that later on in a different context, although the atomic bomb had been developed with the aid of British scientists and sharing all the information had been a critical part of the agreement, the Americans really decided to drop the atomic bomb without consulting the British. They told them they were going to do it but without really consulting and getting their advice. It was at Yalta that Churchill tried to make Roosevelt understand the danger represented by the Soviet Union, that the goal of Stalin was absolute mastery over Eastern Europe. One could not deny the merit of the Soviet army. They had fought bravely—no one wanted to take that away from them—but should we turn Poland over to Russia, his age-old enemy? Had the war not begun to protect the Poles? There was the Polish government, in exile in London, and Churchill fought for them to be given a role in post-war Poland. And Stalin was absolutely clear—no, I will put the government in place, and it will be a communist government. Roosevelt and the Americans were unwilling to challenge—this is the only way it could be challenged ultimately, from a position of absolute strength. So, Poland, Bulgaria, Romania, and ultimately Czechoslovakia would all fall into the grip of odious tyranny—a tyranny that was responsible for more deaths than had ever been inflicted by the Nazis. Churchill had the foresight, but Britain no longer had the power to enforce it.

The next great conference was called in Potsdam in July of 1945. By this time, Franklin Roosevelt, the champion of freedom—as Churchill called him "the best friend Britain ever had"—had died. Harry Truman, a very modest figure in the minds of most, had become president. Churchill liked him the first time they met. He thought Truman might have a stronger sense of what the Soviets were up to than Roosevelt had. They were there together at Potsdam when the general election was held. The results became known. In May of 1945, the Labour Party held its annual convention; there had been a moratorium on a general election during the war. But now Labour said, in May of 1945, we want to go back to party politics, we want an election. And Churchill said, then we shall have one. Churchill's whole life was devoted to parliamentary democracy. He said, behind all the highfalutin words, democracy is about a little man going into a little booth with a little piece of paper, making an "x" upon it, and putting it in to a little box. Let us hold our election.

Churchill began to campaign in late May of 1945. The war with Japan was still raging. He had during the time of the war probably

75-80% of the British people behind him. When victory in Europe was announced on May 8 and May 9, the crowds cheered him. When he spoke to them and said that "evil-doers lie prostrate before us" the crowd literally gasped. "Advance Britannia! Long Live the Cause of Freedom!" he said. He felt confident that he would win the election, but we must recall in Britain's parliamentary democracy—you do not vote for the Prime Minister, you vote for your member of Parliament, and the party that has the largest number of votes wins. Churchill had not only been Minister of Defense and Prime Minister during the war, he had been head of the Conservative Party. Neville Chamberlain died in the fall of 1940; he had been head up until that point, and then Churchill took over the leadership of the Conservative Party. Mrs. Churchill told him, don't do it, it will give a party cast to your decisions, you should stand above party divisions. But Churchill did, he knew from his study of Marlborough what happens to man who does not have party base. So he became head of the Conservative Party and campaigned very vigorously, despite all the other concerns that the war with Japan still on his mind. He ran a campaign of which Mrs. Churchill and his daughter disapproved.

He came out very strongly against the Labour Party and against socialism. He made a speech, and Mrs. Churchill marked out the phrase again and again, and he kept putting it back in, "No Labour government can be established in our country without some form of Gestapo." She kept crossing out "with some for of Gestapo"; he kept putting it back in. It will be a government in which a small party clique as in the Soviet Union controls Parliament like a puppet. It will have to have regimentation to put in place its program of nationalizing railroads, nationalizing the steel industry. There will have to be censorship, and all criticism will have to be stopped. Well, that was not really what the Labour Party was about, but Churchill believed that socialism was the antithesis of democracy. Remember, liberalism was about helping the poor; socialism, he had said from his early days, was about breaking the rich.

But, once again he did not have antennae. The British electorates wanted a change, they had fought through this war, they had been told in the middle of the war that there was a blue print for a new England, for a new Britain, a blue print for education, a blue print for health insurance on a broad scale, a blue print for a welfare state from cradle to grave. That is what the British people wanted. They did not want to return to the Britain before the war. The class system had become odious to them, and for many, despite their admiration for his leadership, Churchill represented that class distinction. His was the idea, in their mind, of noblesse oblige—let us give to the poor, but they don't really deserve it. He didn't think that at all. "Milk for babies is the best investment any government ever makes," that is what he said; that is what he believed. But these long standing hostilities that Labour had for him going back to the Welch miners 35 years before, going back to the general strike. There were also many soldiers who just wanted to come home, and they thought that Churchill "the warmonger" might find some other thing for them to fight. And you would find on bathroom walls, as one of ministers did, going in with General Montgomery, it was scrawled on the wall, "Winston Churchill is a bastard." The minister said that is foul, most foul. And Montgomery said. you have got to understand the men hate politicians.

It was also noted that in victory parades, generals got louder cheers from the troops than Churchill did. As the polling drew near, some generals tried to explain to Churchill, including Lord Mountbatten, his long time friend, he needed to be cautious. The mood of the ordinary soldier was not in favor of the Conservative Party. You have also got understand the Conservative Party had gotten Britain into this mess, had they not? All through the '30s they had been in control, from 1935 onward, they should be highly discredited. This was the party of Stanley Baldwin, and Neville Chamberlain, and Lord Halifax, and so all of these factors came together. Polling was held on July 5, 1945, three weeks would be taken so that all the absentee ballots of the soldiers could be counted. They seem to have done a better job counting the absentee ballots of their soldiers then than with all our technology than we have done in the last election. The votes came in and Churchill was in Potsdam. He came back to London for the votes of the final tally, and almost immediately it became clear that there was a shift. His son lost the election, Randolph lost an election, the son-in-law lost the election, Churchill would be re-elected as a member of Parliament in his district of Epping. But the rest was a Labour landslide and the Conservative Party was turned out.

Churchill went immediately to the king and turned in his seals of office. "At the height of our victory," he would later write, "I was turned out of office." The king suggested that he would make

©2001 The Teaching Company.

Winston a member of the Order of the Garter. And Churchill said, your majesty it would be inappropriate for me to accept the Order of the Garter when I have just got the order of the boot from the British electorates. It was a crushing blow to him, as bad as the Dardanelles. And yet, in the case of the Dardanelles, when he stepped back from it in 1915, he said mistakes were made, I could see why I was blamed, I shouldn't have gotten all the blame, but I can see why. But what had he done wrong now? He had led his people to this great victory. He had worked in concert with Labour. He had worked with Labour to develop a blue print for the future. There was much in the Labour plan of which he approved and would have put in place, but he was out of office.

He went almost immediately to the Continent and began to paint, painting again these bright magnificent visions of a landscape, traveling with members of this family in an entourage. One hundred suitcases and trunks would go along with them. He lived well. General Eisenhower put at his disposal a villa on the Rivera. He stayed with other friends upon the Rivera. But he brooded upon the world's situation. He brooded upon the atomic bomb and what it meant. For now was not only a new tyranny falling over the Europe, but this time mankind had in its hands the opportunity utterly to destroy itself. This time we can bring the world to an end.

In this frame of mind, he came to the United States in March of 1946. He was accompanied by President Truman, they traveled out to Fulton, Missouri, to little Westminster College where he was to be given an honorary degree and made a speech. President Truman read the speech ahead of time and approved of it. And to his audience, Churchill said how honored he was to be given this award, how honored he was that the president had come to introduce him at such an event. Then he spoke about the struggle that had been waged and how it was still not over.

> War and tyranny [he told this audience in Fulton, Missouri] these remain the great enemies of mankind. Have we not seen that this last war nearly brought about a destruction of every aspect of civilization? Do we not understand what war means to the ordinary person? The suffering of men, women, and children as a result of war. Can you not grasp its horror [this from the old soldier, this from the warmonger] and tyranny? Did we fight such a war, undergo such suffering,

that now in large parts of the world, men, women and children still live in fear and in want? Hungry, scared, unable to change their form of government? There is an iron curtain falling across Europe, from Stettin in the Baltic to Trieste in Italy, and behind it many of the most famous capitals of Europe: Bucharest, Sofia, Warsaw. I take nothing away from the bravery of the Russian people in the war. I take nothing away for my wartime college, Marshal Stalin. But we cannot allow this new tyranny to destroy those foundations of freedom that we fought to build.

Now "iron curtain" is just one phrase in it. Probably one-eighth of the speech was taken up with how we must resist this new tyranny. Equally, that much is given over to praising the Soviet Union for what is has done in the war, but the papers leapt upon it. Here is that warmonger again. And the Americans papers took the lead: Churchill has insulted the brave Soviet people; he has caused a crisis where there is not one; he is an alarmist; the Soviets have no desire whatsoever to install their forms of government in Eastern Europe. And President Truman, people like to say that Truman was gutsy person and I guess he was, but as soon as this outcry came, Truman said, I had nothing to do with this speech, I never saw it, and I wouldn't have approved of a speech like that. So, there again, was Churchill alone.

He had a second vision in these years. And then he went to the University of Zurich to receive an honorary degree. When he was at the University of Miami, in Florida, he was receiving an honorary degree, and he looked up over his glasses and said, it always astounds me that for one who failed so many examinations I have received so many degrees. But here he was, getting another degree and he said, I am going to say something today that surprises you. I believe that the only course for us is a United States of Europe, and that at the heart of that United States of Europe must be the coming together of France and Germany. The spirit of France and the spirit of Germany, they must be reunited. In the United States of Europe, all the talent and ability, the capacity of these great parent races will work together for harmony and good and peace.

Ponder that, a United States of Europe, an idea shocking to many there in his audience, and yet it was the vision of the future. It would take more than 50 years to work out, but that is foresight. Already at

 ©2001 The Teaching Company.

Fulton, Missouri he had said to the Americans, I ask of you not an alliance with Britain, I ask for something far deeper and richer, and that is a fraternal alliance. We are not bound by contracts. We are like two brothers with the same ideals. He had this vision of Britain and the United States working together. A United States of Europe, Britain contributing to it, but tied in the closest way to our own country. That was his vision of the future. It is interesting today that when have the United States of Europe. They have chosen a different, less satisfactory name, but the United States of Europe. Then, at the time of tremendous tragedy, on September 11, there was Tony Blair being called by President Bush the best friend America has—Britain.

That vision is still there, still the foundation, and this from a man who first entered Parliament when Victoria was Queen of the British Empire, an empress of India. The Labour government did not turn out to be all the British people had hoped for. By 1951, they were ready for another change; the Conservative Party came back, and with it, Winston Churchill taking over as Prime Minister in the fall of 1951. Now, he is already 77 years of age when he was leading Britain through World War II, we would have had him retired. And now, in the later part of his seventies, he is Prime Minister one more time. During this period he continues to work for the closest possible relations with Americans, making visit after visit to Washington where his old friend Dwight Eisenhower is now president. But he understood that while Britain and America had the same ideals, they do not always have the same interests. Eisenhower and those around him did not share this vision of a fraternal alliance. In fact, for Eisenhower and much of the American administration, the most important thing about Britain was to get rid of its colonial empire. Churchill had said, I did not become First Minister of the King in order to watch over the dismantling of the British Empire. But he also went on and added, somebody else will have to do it, I will not.

That empire was indeed coming to its end. India received its independence while Churchill was out of office. He had long spoken against the independence of India, that it was ready for democracy. It was a land that kept millions of its citizens in the status of being untouchables. He feared for what came about, bloodshed on a large scale, hundreds of thousands of lives lost between Hindus and Muslims, and ultimately, the separation of that country into Pakistan and India. But when it was voted, he was still out of office, and the independence of India became a reality. He called to the leading Indian statesmen, just for a private meeting. He said, now that it is a reality, I will do every thing that I can. I only hope this: that out of independence will come a better life for the ordinary Indian.

Churchill had known that the position of Britain in the world rested upon that great empire. And in the fifties, it was indeed being dismantled in Africa, in the Pacific, but he had a new vision as well. If Britain no longer ruled this great empire, it could still be a moral force. For Churchill, that is what the British Empire had always been about, a moral force. In the 1920s, when a British general had shot down Indians, Churchill spoke out in the most bitter terms against him. He said, if we ever substitute our moral authority for sheer force, then every thing that the British Empire stands for will be as dust.

He wanted Britain to use its moral authority for détente. Yes, this old warmonger and alarmist believed that the atomic bomb had put us in such a situation that there had to be détente between the Soviet Union and the United States. And when Stalin died in 1953, that was the chance. A new government was in power, and he worked again and again on visits to Washington to convince Eisenhower to meet with a new Soviet leadership and start a policy of détente, stop the tensions, and work together. It is just like during the Second World War, they are there and our first priority must be never to have a terrible war. He wasn't listened to, the meeting never came about, the summit he wanted never came about. And Eisenhower wrote in his diary: "Winston was here again, as charming and witty as ever. He wants us to go back to a time during the war when Britain and America were also most as one. That will never be, and those of us who were part of that time knew it was never that way even then. We have the same ideals, but our interests are different."

On April 5, 1955 he stepped down as Prime Minister. The last night he dined with a young queen. He had accepted her wish that he finally become a Knight of the Garter, and he was now Sir Winston Churchill. As he led her to the door, brilliant, vivacious, he said, I began my parliamentary career under Victoria, and it is a special glory to me to be able to say once again, "God Save the Queen." And his last word to his Cabinet: stay close to the Americans.

# Lecture Twelve
# The Legacy of Churchill

**Scope:**

Unlike some recent American politicians, Churchill was not obsessed with his historical legacy. He was content to know that he had done his best. At Churchill's death, Clement Attlee, the socialist who succeeded Churchill as Prime Minister in 1945, called him "the greatest Englishman of our time—I think the greatest citizen of the world of our time." However, in death as in life, Churchill has his critics. Churchill's greatness lay ultimately in his political principles. What did Churchill understand by *liberty* and *democracy*? What role did he see for government in securing individual and political freedom? How did Churchill reconcile his love of liberty with his belief in the British Empire and his view of the beneficent influence of British imperialism? What were the sources of these political principles, and where does he stand in the great liberal tradition, reaching back to Magna Carta and classical antiquity? How did he unswervingly uphold these principles over a political life of more than 50 tumultuous years?

# Outline

I.  As Prime Minister from 1951–1955, Churchill had worked for détente and carried a bold vision for a united Europe. He understood that the British people wanted their cradle-to-grave welfare state. He had never been opposed to many of the welfare benefits they desired.

   A.  His last years saw growing honors and failing health.

   B.  In 1953, he received the Nobel Prize for Literature.

   C.  Also in 1953, he finally agreed to his monarch's wish that he be knighted and, thus, became Sir Winston Churchill.

   D.  He remained a member of Parliament until 1964, when he was 89 years old.

   E.  He continued to paint and remained interested in his hobbies, including horse racing, tropical fish, and pigs.

   F.  He traveled frequently.

**G.** His *History of the Second World War* brought him a fortune and the Nobel Prize.

**H.** His *History of the English-Speaking Peoples* was equally successful.

**I.** Personal tragedy struck him in 1963 when his daughter Diana died.

**J.** He was very supportive of his children, especially of his son, Randolph.

**K.** He was not worried about his legacy but was content that he had done his best.

**II.** Churchill's political philosophy was rooted in the ideal of freedom.

    **A.** The source for Churchill's ideals was the great tradition of English liberty, stretching back to Magna Carta and beyond. He defined freedom in concrete terms.

        **1.** Does a people have the right to criticize its government, and can it change a government whenever it wishes?

        **2.** Are the courts and legal system fair and open, and do the poor have the same right as the rich to a fair court trial?

        **3.** Does the ordinary citizen have the right to live without fear of arbitrary arrest?

    **B.** Churchill agreed with Franklin Roosevelt that true liberty was "freedom to worship, freedom to speak, freedom from fear, and freedom from want."

    **C.** He saw World War I as a great struggle for individual liberty.

    **D.** For Churchill, society must have economic opportunity and free trade, but with these, there must be security for individuals from the loss of a job, from an old age without funds, from sickness without medical care.

    **E.** He believed that parliamentary democracy was the true guardian of individual liberty.

    **F.** Churchill was, at heart, a profound democrat.

    **G.** How can his imperialism be accommodated to his belief in democracy?

        **1.** For Churchill, the British Empire supported individual liberty. He did not believe that national independence and freedom were the same thing. He did not see freedom in turning over a country to a small clique of its own that would rule in absolute tyranny over others.

**2.** He believed that for every freedom, there was also a responsibility.

**3.** For Churchill, British law and administration offered protection to the many minorities in India, and the British tradition of liberty under law offered the best guidance for the future development of India.

**H.** He was a Zionist from his earliest days in Parliament.

**I.** He believed that a politician and a statesman must set priorities.

**J.** Although he understood the horrors of war, he also understood that there were times when war had to be fought; some ideologies existed that only recognized strength.

**K.** He believed that negotiation must always come from a position of strength (both military might and moral authority).

**III.** Churchill never lacked for critics in his own day, and historians have never left him alone. Churchill is still controversial.

**A.** Some biographers and historians praise Churchill as the greatest individual of the 20th century, who saved freedom. Others regard him as a failure and the foe of liberty.

**B.** In 1966, the distinguished British historian A. J. P. Taylor published a collection of essays on Churchill, *Churchill Revised: A Critical Assessment.* It includes essays by Basil Liddell Hart, who regarded Churchill as a failed statesman and strategist.

**C.** Robert Rhodes James, in his 1970 biography, *Churchill: A Study in Failure, 1900–1939,* and John Charmley, in his 1993 biography, *Churchill: The End of Glory,* both attack Churchill as a failure in almost everything he did.

**D.** For Charmley, Taylor, and others, the essence of Churchill's failure lies in the fact that World War II destroyed Britain's power.

**1.** In their eyes, Churchill had wanted to make Britain great, but in the end, Britain was a third-rate power indebted to the United States.

**2.** They find Churchill outwitted by Roosevelt.

3. They believe that the demands Churchill made on Britain's resources crippled the country.

4. They also focus on the fact that he left power at the time of the Dardanelles, was out of power again during the 1930s, and that his second term of office as Prime Minister achieved almost nothing—all the result of personal flaws in Churchill, including his impetuosity and his inability to judge the public mood.

E. But Churchill did not define World War II as a struggle to make Britain great. His goal was not to expand the British Empire; it was, as he himself said repeatedly, a war for freedom.

F. In 1947, Churchill dreamed of seeing Europe restored to a position of power. Today, the European Union fulfills that dream, with its intellect and its resources, all proceeding under peace, individual liberty, and parliamentary democracy, and Britain is an integral part of that Europe.

G. Churchill strove for that kind of freedom, where the individual is better off than before. He rallied Britain to stand alone at a time when totalitarianism was rampant from Spain to Russia.

H. Shortly before his death, Churchill's daughter Mary wrote him: "In addition to the feeling a daughter has for a loving generous father, I owe you what every Englishman, woman, and child does, liberty itself.

IV. On January 10, 1965, Churchill suffered a massive stroke. Two weeks later he was dead.

A. He received a state funeral at St. Paul's Cathedral; 300,000 people visited his coffin.

B. As his body was taken down the River Thames to the gravesite, workmen along the river raised their cranes in solitary salute.

C. He was buried in the family cemetery at Bladon, near Blenheim Palace.

**Essential Reading:**

Blake and Louis, *Churchill.*

Gilbert, *Churchill's Political Philosophy.*

Taylor, *Churchill Revised.*

**Supplementary Reading:**

Barrett, *Churchill: Concise Bibliography.*

Halle, *Irrepressible Churchill.*

Rasor, *Churchill: Comprehensive Bibliography.*

**Questions to Consider:**

1. Consider Churchill's definition of a tyrant: A tyrant is one who places his own ideas and desires above the good of ordinary people. Why were he and Roosevelt fundamentally different from Stalin and Hitler?

2. How near are we now to Churchill's vision of the world?

# Lecture Twelve—Transcript
## The Legacy of Churchill

In our last lecture, we saw Winston Churchill as Prime Minister a second time—from 1951 until April 5, 1955. Shortly after he laid down his office, he went to Sicily. He was painting there in Syracuse and wrote a letter to the queen that he was looking down upon the quarries in Syracuse, where the Athenians had been held as prisoners so many centuries before the collapse of the great Athenian armada in 413 B.C., the legacy of history weighing heavy. But I am content, he said, simply to know that I have done my best. He wasn't worried about a legacy because he had done his best. He had done his best during the war. He had done his best as Prime Minister the second time, and his time as Prime Minister from 1951 to 1955 was not a period of stagnation. His bold vision of a united Europe, his hope for détente, and the simple fact that he understood that the British people wanted their new cradle-to-grave welfare state. He did not try to reverse and go back to the past. He had never been opposed to many of these welfare benefits. So he remained one of the architects of the modern welfare state. He would not have been ashamed of that title.

His health had not been good, already on a visit to Washington during the Second World War he had suffered a heart attack, and in 1953, while Prime Minister, he had quiet a severe stroke, but he recovered from it. Many in the Conservative Party, at the highest levels of leadership, were eager for him to step down—none more so that Anthony Eden. Eden was a brave man, and he went right from Eaton College to the trenches of WWI. He was highly decorated. He had resigned from the Cabinet over Chamberlain's policy of appeasement, and he looked upon himself as Churchill's heir. But Churchill, partly just to spite, him stayed on another year after his stroke, and Eden became more and more impatient. He finally got to be Prime Minister, and within two years was sucked into the crisis of the Suez Canal. Remember the Egyptians nationalized the Suez Canal, the British and French invaded, and there was such an uproar and complete lack of support, and indeed opposition from the Americans, that Eden had to step down as Prime Minister.

Churchill was consulted about his successor, and he, like others, suggested Harold McMillan, but that was his main role after he had retired, though he stayed on as a member of Parliament until 1963. He stayed on representing Parliament—going on a fairly regular

 ©2001 The Teaching Company.

basis. He spent much of his time painting. He would go to the Rivera about three months out of the year. His skills as a painter remained strong. It was in this period that he painted that magnificent portrait of Mrs. Churchill, as she had been in 1940, launching a ship. He kept his interest in life by well-rounded hobbies. In 1951, again to the absolute dismay of Mrs. Churchill, he took up horse racing and brought out of mothballs his father's old colors: pink and brown. Not only did he take up horse racing, but for once he was successful at gambling, and his horses made quite a bit of money, including the Winston Churchill Stakes that had been named after him. He took up an interest in tropical fish. He had always loved goldfish, but now he took up one in tropical fishes. He would jump up in the middle of a luncheon to feed his fish. Pigs, he took up with pigs and began to raise pigs. Again, Mrs. Churchill did not like this idea, she was always trying to turn them into bacon. She once was going to kill a goose, and he said, Clemmie, it is a friend, if you kill it, I won't eat it. So he took up with these pigs—remember, cats look on people, dogs look up at people, and pigs just treat us as equals—so he had these little pigs.

One of the most endearing portraits to me is of Churchill standing by one of his fishponds with the look of deep sadness on his face and someone said, what has happened? He said, I cannot find my little goldfish. He was poking in it with his walking stick. There he is, on another occasion, he said, where are the ducklings? They were here yesterday. Now the mother is swimming by herself. It is the toads who have done it—the toads have eaten the ducklings—let us build a wall to keep the toads out. Then suddenly, the mother duck raised her little wings and there were all the babies under there, safe, they were well. What a loving man, I just think these are wonderful portraits of him.

He liked, in particular, the company of Aristotle Onassis. This was before Onassis, the great shipping magnate, had married Jacqueline Kennedy. He would spend a lot of time on the yacht of Aristotle Onassis; he took eight voyages with Aristotle Onassis. Onassis put in a pool on the yacht, a swimming pool just for Churchill, and Churchill would claim in his later years that only Onassis could understand what he said and only he could understand what Onassis said. So people would sit there trying to talk to Churchill and say I am sorry, and Onassis would interpret, he would then speak back in a soft voice to Onassis, and he would give an answer. And so they sailed around the Mediterranean on the yacht, *Christina*. Or he would stay with friends at their villas, like his great friend and literary agent in America, Emery Reves, who had come originally from Hungary.

He wrote and published. He had an enormous income. His *History of the Second World War*, his memoirs essentially, had brought him a fortune and the Nobel Prize. Then, a work that he had been completing as WWII broke out, and put it on the shelf until he could go back to it, his *History of the English-Speaking Peoples*, that statement of America and Britain as the great mothers of parliamentary democracy and of freedom. There are two wonderful chapters on the American Civil War, and he would visit the battlefields at Gettysburg. It was a publishing phenomenon and brought him an enormous income. And yet he still worried about money.

You know, when people ask if Churchill was a success, I think we ought to go step by step and see what he achieved. Now, he was a member of Parliament at the age of 26. If you want to say it is important just to stay in office, he stayed in office all those years, only being out of Parliament two years. Now that is successful as a politician. He reached high office, and by 1929, he had already served five years as Chancellor of the Exchequer. Well, to be Chancellor of the Exchequer is something, the second highest office in Britain, and then twice to be Prime Minister. So I think that is real success as a politician. Now, he was also a successful author. Don't you think winning the Nobel Prize is a statement of success as an author? Don't you think making more than a million dollars in our currency, year after year, from your writings is a success? We have seen his paintings come to hang in the Tate Gallery, to decorate the royal collection, to bring in a considerable income, to win prizes under a pseudonym.

But he was also a good businessman, and there is nothing wrong with making money. By the time he was 26, he was a millionaire in our terms. He was always a shrewd bargainer. Now he wasn't very good at gambling. One of the reasons he like to go the Rivera was to gamble at Monte Carlo, Mrs. Churchill was utterly opposed to this, he almost always lost. And he lost gambling in the stock market in 1929—he remade that money—but by 1938, he invested again very heavily and there was another dip in the Americans stock market, and not only had he lost £15,000, he owed £18,000. He said to friends, I am going to have to resign from Parliament and devote myself entirely to writing. And sure enough, his friends went to friends in the city, the financial area of London, and found those who were willing to buy up Churchill's fallen securities at the price he had originally paid for, to manage them for him for three years with a proviso that he did not make any more investments, and so he came out that financial disaster.

Now, there is nothing wrong taking care of your family. In 1946, again he said, I have money worries, and I no longer have my salary as Prime Minister, I think I am going to have sell Chartwell—this to his old-time friend, Lord Camrose. You cannot sell Chartwell. I know it would be the death of me, but what can I do? What if we paid you three million dollars (£50,000 pounds in those days)? You can have Chartwell and "I will throw the corpse in with it"—you can bury me here. So, it was worked out: he was paid the equivalent of three million dollars, he could live at Chartwell for just a nominal rent for the rest of his life, and then it would go to the National Trust where it remains today. Now that is a sharp business deal. I see nothing wrong with doing it. He could live on in quite and peace there in his beloved Chartwell. He knew how to make money and provide for his family.

Still time passed on and it brought with it sadness as well. His daughter, Diana, had long been depressed and in 1963 committed suicide. At first he could not understand what was being told him, and then he withdrew to a deep silence. His son Randolph admired Churchill enormously, he wanted to be like Churchill but he wasn't. He ran four times for Parliament and lost. He wrote two volumes of his father's biography, and I think they are splendidly written. But he drank, his father could carry the alcohol, Randolph could not. He was an alcoholic and would die young, in very, very bad health from sclerosis of the liver. He would out live his father, but Randolph was a disappointment to Churchill, but he never told him such. He tried throughout his life to support him, and indeed, Mrs. Churchill would say over and over to Winston, you are ruining Randolph, you must be stricter with him. He could not be strict. He didn't approve of his daughter Sarah's first husband, Vic Oliver, a music hall entertainer. And once, when somebody said, what a terrible fall Mussolini has had. Churchill said, yes, but at least he got to shoot his son-in-law. So, not everything was happy for him. But he lived on.

He grew deaf, and once he was leaving Parliament, and there were these young M.P.s walking behind him, and they were snickering, I hear the old fellow has gone gaga. And he stopped and turned around, and said, yes, I hear he had gone quite deaf too. Nobody put much over on him. Mrs. Churchill worried about his getting increasingly old, and she indeed convinced him to finally give up his seat in Parliament. But one of his favorite things in these final years was to go to his old school, Harrow, to what was the equivalent of their commencement exercises. He was there at Harrow and Mrs. Churchill had said, don't go, you are just not up to it. And indeed, the headmaster worried because Churchill sat there and slept all during most of the ceremonies. But when he was introduced, he got up and walked out and looked out over those boys and said simply: Never give up, never, never, never. You will never hear a better commencement address than that or better advice from any of us, no matter what our age.

His was a legacy, and without worrying about his historical legacy, he has left to ages to come, I would say, a most enduring legacy of greatness. His political philosophy was rooted in the ideal of freedom. That was the wellspring of all of Mr. Winston Churchill's actions, so said his private secretary. He defined this freedom for us. Does, he said, the people have the right to turn out its government? In other words, it is first of all political freedom. Do you have the right to criticize government openly? Do you have the right to open elections, and can you change the government when it is necessary, when you want to—that is the first step. Then secondly, there has to be justice. The courts have to be open and the poor person must have the same right to a fair trial as the wealthy. And the courts must not be under any political pressure. These are simple ideals, but they are at the very root of what you mean by freedom. Then, does the ordinary person have the right to live, earn his living, raise his children without being afraid of arbitrary arrest, simply hauled off in the night. He would have agreed with President Roosevelt: freedom of worship, freedom of speech, freedom from fear, freedom from want, those are the most basic elements of individual freedom.

He saw the Second World War as a great struggle for individual liberty. There must be also economic opportunities. He believed his entire life in free trade and a free market economy. He had broken with the Conservative Party over tariffs. Free trade, economic opportunity, but with it the security of the ordinary person, individuals, small man, from the loss of his job, from an old age without funds, from sickness without medical care. So that was individual freedom for him, and the freedom for which this great war had been fought.

He believed also that Britain was the mother of such freedom. It stretched back to Magna Charta, to Habeas Corpus, it stretched back to the Glorious Revolution of 1688, in which his ancestor, Marlborough, had played such an important role. Parliamentary democracy: that was the true guardian of individual liberty. He saw much pride in the fact that Abraham Lincoln, a statue of him, looked out on Parliament. The American Civil War was in his bones; it had been a struggle about freedom and democracy. And Churchill was at heart a profound democrat.

Now, how do you reconcile this with his belief in the British Empire? To us, it is impossible in our own day. Imperialism is a word fraught only with negative connotations. But not only had he grown up in an era when imperialism was a good word, when the empire was a grand thing, he never gave up that view. And it was not an anachronism. To him, the British Empire had supported individual liberty. He did not believe that national independence and freedom were the same thing. He did not see freedom in turning a country over to a small clique of its own, who would then rule with absolute ruthlessness and tyranny over others. He would have been appalled at the genocide that we have witnessed in countries in our own day. He would have said, that is not freedom, that is shirking a moral responsibility. And in the '30s, when the empire had become a burden to the British, and in the late '40s and '50s, when they were dismantling it, his voice rose up and said, but you cannot give up a moral responsibility. We took over the rule of these people, now we must guide and see that their independence is worth having, that there are true democracies established. That is not happened all over, in what was once the colonial world, I think we must agree.

So for him, the burden of empire was part of the responsibility of freedom. You see, he believed that for every freedom there was also a responsibility. He had begun with the great freedom of his birth as an Englishman; he had been born into a class that made it possible for him to rise to the top. So he assumed the awesome responsibilities that came with it. Freedom, empire: these were essential to his political fiber. He was, he said from his earliest days in Parliament, a Zionist. He saw in the struggle of the Jewish people to obtain their holy land, a homeland for themselves, he saw in it an unfolding of freedom and of justice. After the Second World War, when the true horrors of the Holocaust had come home to the world, he believed even more strongly that Israel must be a nation and that there, in the homeland, the Jews must have a place of rest and quite and peace. He would have wondered about attempts to settle that in our own day, in our own moment, that might strip away from the Jewish people the very fabric of their security. He always believed that a politician, a statesman, must set priorities and sometimes this meant saying no to the aspirations of one people for another.

Churchill also understood so very, very deeply that war itself had, at times, to be fought. You must preserve strength, and that there were nations, there were people, there were ideologies that recognized only strength. He understood the horror of war. War, he said, that was once squalid and glorious is now just squalid, but at times it must be fought. So negotiate, he would say to us, always from a position of strength, and that strength is both guns as well as moral authority.

Churchill never lacked for critics in his own parliamentary career. And time and time again he was attacked: unscrupulous, an adventurer, an opportunist, a failure. And the historians have not let him alone. He was barely dead when a book was published in 1966, *Churchill Revised: A Critical Assessment,* a collection of essays put together by the very distinguished British historian, A. J. P. Taylor. It included essays on Churchill as a strategist by the famous British military historian, Basil Liddell Hart. He was highly critical of Churchill. Churchill, in his view, was a failure as a statesman, he was a failure as a strategist, and there is a most influential school of historical thought today that views Churchill as a failure. John Charmley's biography of Churchill, published in 1993, *Churchill: The End of Glory,* is a scathing attack upon Churchill. Well documented, full of narrative: it still somehow reminds me of an essay in character assassination. Almost everything Churchill did is put in the worst possible light.

But for both A. J. P. Taylor and Charmley, and others, the essence of Churchill's failure lies in the fact that the Second World War destroyed the power of Britain, and so they tried to define this in Churchill's own terms. He had wanted to make the British Empire

          ©2001 The Teaching Company.

great, and at the end, Britain was a third-rate power indebted to the United States. They find Churchill outwitted by Roosevelt. They find that the demand he made upon the national resources of Britain crippled it. And of course, they also focus on the fact that he left power at the time of the Dardanelles, he was kept out of office all during the 1930s, and his second time as a Prime Minister he did almost nothing. All of these are due to personal flaws in Churchill— the kind we looked at in our lecture on the Dardanelles: his impetuosity, his inability to judge the public mood—all of these render him a failure.

In the first place, Churchill did not define the Second World War as a struggle to make Britain great. His goal was not the expansion of the British Empire; it was, as he said over and over again to the British people, it was a war for freedom. It was a war to establish the temple of individual rights and a foundation that could not be shaken. Let us keep that in mind. These academic historians have an attitude, I think, that only professors can really grasp. Their idea is that Churchill somehow must be like a dean who just stays in office, that is his job, to stay in office year after year and not to make any hard decisions. That is not how Churchill ever saw politics. It is how Stanley Baldwin saw it, it is how Neville Chamberlain saw it, but he saw politics as the opportunity to do what was right.

You see, for these historians, there are no absolute rights, there is nothing absolutely right and there is nothing absolutely wrong. We do not believe in truth any more, and we don't believe in absolute justice. We live in a society in which the lie is the norm, and there are only shades of lying, and you only get in trouble if you get caught lying. So, politicians will lie all the time. We all lie all the time. Churchill did not. There were absolute truths, absolute right and wrong, and that is what you fought for. So, you see, if you cut out that foundation from Churchill, if you say nothing is worth an ultimate struggle because nothing is that important in the end, then of course you judge him as a failure.

But, even in those terms, was he a failure? I want you to think of something. Today more people live in freedom than ever before— more democracy, more freedom than ever before. And out of the carnage of Europe has come that united Europe of which Churchill spoke. He dreamed in 1947 of seeing Europe with all its ancient glories once again restored to a position of power. Is that not true now? The European Union, with its industrious population, its intellect, its resources, is the equal of our own country. And it is all proceeding under peace, individual liberty, and parliamentary democracy. I do not see Britain as a destroyed power but as an intricate part of that Europe. And Churchill would have said, I did my best and that is my true legacy. A Britain that is free, where the ordinary person lives a better life than ever before—and all of this as part of this Europe, is that failure? You would have to be a professor to somehow see failure in that, to so ignore the simple facts, and without Winston Churchill that would not be. He rallied Britain to stand alone at a time when a totalitarian government stretched from the Pillars of Hercules and Franco-Spain all the way out to Vladivostok in Stalin's Russia.

On the 10th of January, in 1965, Churchill suffered a massive stroke. Two weeks later he was dead. Three hundred thousand filed by his coffin as it lay in state. As it was carried down the streets of London, soldiers from both wars came out to salute him. It was loaded on a little tug and taken down the Thames River. We have seen how many times he quarreled with labor, but at that moment the working men along the Thames, on their own, raised up their cranes in solitary salute. He was taken back to Blenheim, the little village right outside the gates of Bladon, and laid to rest there beside his father and mother. Shortly before he died, his daughter, Mary, wrote to him: "Not only do I owe what every daughter owes a loving and devoted father, I owe what every Englishman, woman, and child owes you, liberty itself." And we, as Americans, can pay that same tribute to Winston Churchill.

 ©2001 The Teaching Company.

# Excerpts from Churchill's Speeches

## Lecture One
## From a Speech to the House of Commons, June 4, 1940

Even though large tracts of Europe and many old and famous States have fallen or may fall into the grip of the Gestapo and all the odious apparatus of Nazi rule, we shall not flag or fail. We shall go on to the end, we shall fight in France, we shall fight on the seas and oceans, we shall fight with growing confidence and growing strength in the air, we shall defend our island whatever the cost may be, we shall fight on the beaches, we shall fight on the landing grounds, we shall fight in the fields and in the streets, we shall fight in the hills; we shall never surrender and even if, which I do not for a moment believe, this island or a large part of it were subjugated and starving, then our Empire beyond the seas, armed and guarded by the British Fleet, would carry on the struggle, until in God's good time, the new world, with all its power and might, steps forth to the rescue and the liberation of the old.

## Lecture Eight
## From a Speech to the House of Commons, October 5, 1938

I do not begrudge our loyal, brave people, who were ready to do their duty no matter what the cost, who never flinched under the strain of last week—I do not grudge them the natural, spontaneous outburst of joy and relief when they learned that the hard ordeal would no longer be required of them at the moment; but they should know the truth. They should know that there has been gross neglect and deficiency in our defences; they should know that we have sustained a defeat without a war, the consequences of which will travel far with us along our road; they should know that we have passed an awful milestone in our history, when the whole equilibrium of Europe has been deranged, and that the terrible words have for the time being been pronounced against the Western democracies: "Thou art weighed in the balance and found wanting." And do not suppose that this is the end. This is only the beginning of the reckoning. This is only the first sip, the first foretaste of a bitter cup which will be proffered to us year by year unless by a supreme recovery of moral health and martial vigour, we arise again and take our stand for freedom as in the olden time.

**Lecture Nine**
**From a Speech to the House of Commons, May 13, 1940**

I would say to the House, as I said to those who have joined the Government: "I have nothing to offer but blood, toil, tears and sweat."

We have before us an ordeal of the most grievous kind. We have before us many, many long months of struggle and of suffering. You ask, what is our policy? I will say: It is to wage war, by sea, land and air, with all our might and with all the strength that God can give us: to wage war against a monstrous tyranny, never surpassed in the dark, lamentable catalogue of human crime. That is our policy. You ask, What is our aim? I can answer in one word: Victory—victory at all costs, victory in spite of all terror, victory, however long and hard the road may be; for without victory, there is no survival. Let that be realized; no survival for the British Empire; no survival for all that the British Empire has stood for, no survival for the urge and impulse of the ages, that mankind will move forward towards its goal. But I take up my task with buoyancy and hope. I feel sure that our cause will not be suffered to fail among men. At this time I feel entitled to claim the aid of all, and I say, "Come, then, let us go forward together with our united strength."

**Lecture Ten**
**From a Speech to the House of Commons, June 18, 1940**

What General Weygand called the Battle of France is over. I expect that the Battle of Britain is about to begin. Upon this battle depends the survival of Christian civilization. Upon it depends our own British life, and the long continuity of our institutions and our Empire. The whole fury and might of the enemy must very soon be turned on us. Hitler knows that he will have to break us in this island or lose the war. If we can stand up to him, all Europe may be free and the life of the world may move forward into broad, sunlit uplands. But if we fail, then the whole world, including the United States, including all that we have known and cared for, will sink into the abyss of a new Dark Age made more sinister, and perhaps more protracted, by the lights of perverted science. Let us therefore brace ourselves to our duties and so bear ourselves that, if the British Empire and its Commonwealth last for a thousand years, men will still say, "This was their finest hour."

    ©2001 The Teaching Company.

## Lecture Twelve
## From the Iron Curtain Speech at Fulton, Missouri, March 5, 1946

But we must never cease to proclaim in fearless tones the great principles of freedom and the rights of man which are the joint inheritance of the English-speaking world and which through Magna Carta, the Bill of Rights, the Habeas Corpus, trial by jury, and the English common law find their most famous expression in the American Declaration of Independence.

All this means that the people of any country have the right, and should have the power by constitutional action, by free unfettered elections, with secret ballot, to choose or change the character or form of government under which they dwell; that freedom of speech and thought should reign; that courts of justice, independent of the executive, unbiased by any part, should administer laws which have received the broad assent of large majorities or are consecrated by time and custom. Here are the title deeds of freedom which should lie in every cottage home. Here is the message of the British and American peoples to mankind. Let us preach what we practice—let us practice what we preach.

# Maps

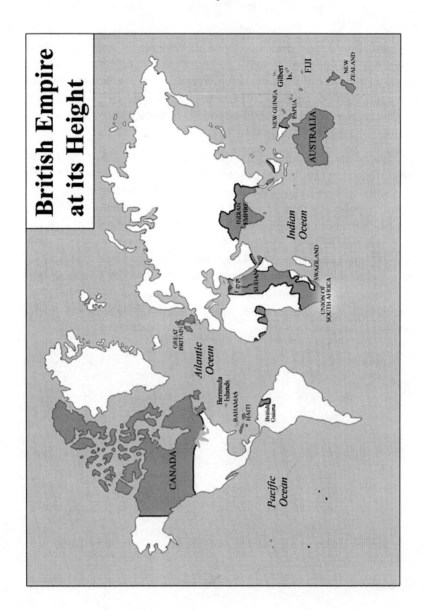

©2001 The Teaching Company.

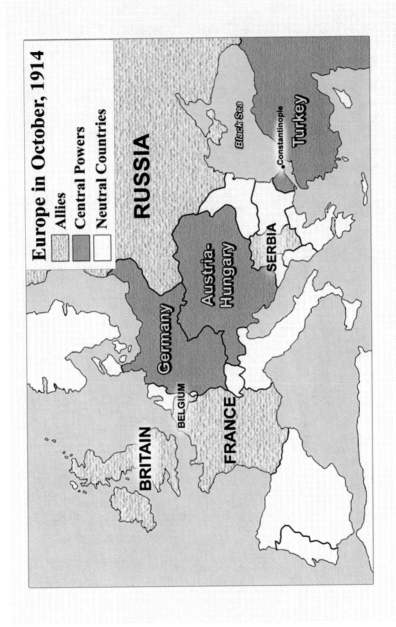

Europe in October, 1914

Allies
Central Powers
Neutral Countries

BRITAIN
BELGIUM
FRANCE
Germany
Austria-Hungary
SERBIA
RUSSIA
Black Sea
Constantinople
Turkey

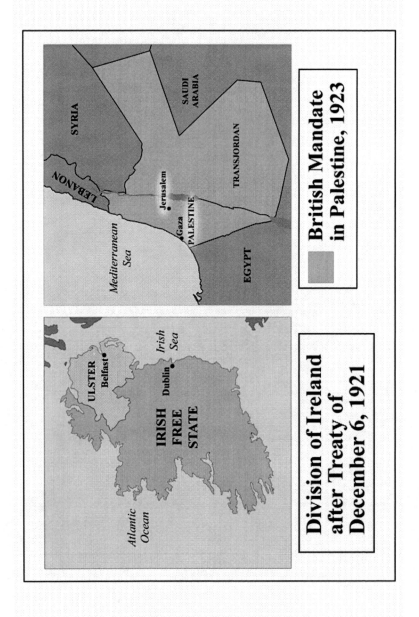

British Mandate
in Palestine, 1923

Division of Ireland
after Treaty of
December 6, 1921

©2001 The Teaching Company.

## Map Legend

- Soviet Controlled Territory, 1939-40
- Axis Territory, Sept. 1939
- Axis Occupied Territory, w/ dates of occupation
- Neutral Countries
- Allied Territory
- Axis Satellites

# German Expansion, 1939-1941

NORWAY

SWEDEN

Invasion of Norway April-June 1940

BRITAIN

Denmark

Atlantic Ocean

Evacuation of Dunkirk, May 1940

Holland

Belgium

Invasion of Denmark, April, 1940

Invasion of France and Low Countries, May 1940

Invasion of Poland, Sept. 1939

FRANCE

GERMANY

POLAND

U.S.S.R.

VICHY FRANCE (1940-42)

Switz.

Invasion of Yugoslavia, April, 1941

Slovakia

HUNGARY

ITALY

YUGOSLAVIA

ROMANIA

Black Sea

BULGARIA

AID

Invasion of Greece, April 1941

Mediterranean Sea

GREECE

MOROCCO

Sicily

ALGERIA

Vichy Controlled (1940-42)

TUNISIA

Mediterranean Sea

Suez Canal

Landing Afrika Korps, Feb. 1941

LIBYA

British Egypt

# Timeline

1650–1722.................................John Churchill, First Duke of Marlborough.

1849–1895................................Lord Randolph Churchill.

November 30, 1874....................Birth of Winston Churchill.

1874 .........................................Randolph Churchill entered Parliament.

1886 .........................................Randolph Churchill Chancellor of the Exchequer and Leader of House of Commons; resigned as Chancellor of Exchequer; beginning of his political and physical decline.

1888 .........................................Churchill enrolled in Harrow for secondary school education.

1893–1894................................Received military education at Royal Military College, Sandhurst.

1895 .........................................Visited America and began his career as a journalist and war correspondent in Cuba.

1896 .........................................Posted to India as subaltern (lieutenant) in Fourth Hussars.

1897 .........................................In action against Afghan tribesmen on northwest frontier of India.

1898 .........................................Published his first book, *The Story of the Malakand Field Force*, and took part in the Battle of Omdurman in the Sudan.

1899 .........................................Lost his first attempt at election to Parliament; published his second book, *The River War*; participated in the Boer War and was taken prisoner; his escape made him a national hero.

©2001 The Teaching Company.

| 1900 | Elected to Parliament as a member of the Conservative Party. |
|------|----------------------------------------------------------------|
| 1904 | Joined the Liberal Party. |
| 1905 | Appointed Under Secretary for Colonial Affairs, his first government post. |
| 1906 | Published biography of Lord Randolph Churchill. |
| 1908 | Married Clementine Hozier and appointed President of the Board of Trade, making him a member of the Cabinet. |
| 1910 | Appointed Home Secretary; acted decisively to put down riots by striking miners but refused to use army troops to do so. |
| 1911 | Appointed First Lord of the Admiralty. |
| 1914–1918 | World War I. |
| 1915 | Churchill was the driving force behind development of the tank and the Dardanelles campaign; resigned as First Lord of the Admiralty. |
| 1916 | As colonel, commanded Sixth Royal Scots Fusiliers in action on western front. |
| 1917 | Cleared by Dardanelles Commission investigation; received position in the government as Minister of Munitions. |
| 1919 | Appointed Secretary of State for War; urged armed intervention against Bolsheviks. |
| 1921 | Appointed Colonial Secretary; supported creation of Jewish |

homeland; played major role in negotiations that led ultimately to establishment of the Republic of Ireland.

1922 ...........................................Mussolini seized power in Italy.

1922 ...........................................Churchill bought country home, Chartwell.

1922–1924.................................Defeated in three straight elections; out of Parliament.

1923–1931.................................Published *The World Crisis*, his five-volume memoirs of World War I.

1924 ...........................................Elected to Parliament from town of Epping, supported by Conservative Party; held this seat in Parliament for the rest of his career, until 1964; appointed Chancellor of the Exchequer (Secretary of the Treasury).

1925 ...........................................Rejoined the Conservative Party; as Chancellor of the Exchequer, returned Britain to the gold standard.

1926 ...........................................Decisive action during general strike further embittered Churchill's relations with labor unions.

1929 ...........................................Conservative Party lost election; Churchill out of office but remained in Parliament; lost fortune in stock market crash.

1930 ...........................................Published his autobiography, *My Early Life*; Broke with Conservative Party leadership over India.

1931–1939.................................In the political wilderness, in Parliament but out of favor with his Conservative Party; Roosevelt became President of the United States; Hitler became Chancellor of Germany.

1936 .........................................Germany remilitarized the Rhineland.

1938 .........................................Germany annexed Austria; Munich Conference and British and French betrayal of Czechoslovakia; Neville Chamberlain promised British "peace in out time."

1939 .........................................German invasion of Poland; Churchill appointed First Lord of the Admiralty.

1940 .........................................Churchill appointed Prime Minister; fall of France; Battle of Britain.

1941 .........................................Germany invaded the Soviet Union; United States entered the war.

1942 .........................................Japanese captured Singapore; Battle of Stalingrad; British victory at El Alamein; Allied invasion of North Africa.

1943 .........................................Allied conquest of Sicily; fall of Mussolini; Italy signed armistice with Allies; conference at Teheran.

1944 .........................................Normandy invasion.

1945 .........................................Conference at Yalta; suicide of Hitler; Germany surrendered; conference at Potsdam; Churchill and Conservative Party defeated in election; Japan surrendered.

1946 .........................................Churchill made Iron Curtain speech at Fulton, Missouri; promoted idea of European unity.

1948–1954................................Published six-volume memoirs, *The Second World War.*

©2001 The Teaching Company.

| | |
|---|---|
| 1951–1955 | Served second term as Prime Minister. |
| 1953 | Received the Nobel Prize for Literature and made a Knight of the Garter; henceforth, he was Sir Winston Churchill. |
| 1956–1958 | Published his *History of the English-Speaking Peoples.* |
| 1963 | Was made the first honorary citizen of the United States. |
| 1964 | Ended his parliamentary career by refusing to stand for reelection. |
| January 24, 1965 | Churchill died. |

 ©2001 The Teaching Company.

# Glossary

**Admiralty, First Lord of**: As First Lord of the Admiralty from 1911 to 1915 and again from 1939 to 1940, Churchill was in charge of the maintenance and administration of the British navy and of policies regarding the navy and the British Empire by sea.

**Blenheim Palace**: Palatial residence built (1704–1722) at public expense by Queen Anne and Parliament as home for John Churchill, First Duke of Marlborough. It is still the home of the Dukes of Marlborough.

**Board of Trade**: A department of the British government charged with advising the government on commercial policy. As President of the Board of Trade in 1908, Churchill became a member of the Cabinet.

**Boer or South African War**: Bloody struggle (1899–1902) for independence from Britain by Boers or Afrikaners (descendants of Dutch settlers). The British won, but the Afrikaners achieved many of their goals in the resulting settlement, in which Churchill played a significant role.

**British Empire**: When Churchill entered Parliament in 1900, Britain, a nation the size of Colorado, ruled an empire on which the sun never set, stretching from the Arctic Circle to New Zealand and from Ireland to Fiji, and including India and a good portion of Africa.

**Chancellor of the Exchequer**: In charge of the treasury and budget, the Chancellor of the Exchequer is second in importance to the Prime Minister. The position is frequently regarded as a stepping stone to becoming Prime Minister. When Churchill presented his budget to Parliament in 1929, he was one of the longest serving Chancellors of the Exchequer in British history. The others all became Prime Minister, as did Churchill: Walpole, Peel, Pitt, and Gladstone.

**Chartwell**: Churchill's country home from 1922 to 1965. See Lecture Four.

**Colonial Secretary**: This office dealt with matters relating to British dependent territories. As Undersecretary of State for the Colonies from 1905 to 1908, Churchill was involved in the settlement of issues in South Africa. As Colonial Secretary from 1921 to 1922,

Churchill played a prominent role in questions of the Middle East and Ireland.

**Conservative Party**: The Conservative Party is the descendant of the Tory Party of the 17th and 18th centuries. It stood originally for the monarch against Parliament. By 1830, the term *Conservative Party* came into general use, although it has never entirely replaced *Tory*. Disraeli (1804–1881) was the Conservative counterpart to Gladstone. The Conservatives supported British imperialism. Conservative opposition to Home Rule for Ireland led to an influx of supporters from the Liberal Party (the Unionists) after 1886. The Conservatives supported social legislation in the later part of the 19th century and into the 20th. The Conservatives also supported tariffs, which led Churchill to leave the Conservative Party in 1904. See also Lecture Three.

**Dardanelles Campaign**: See Lecture Three.

**Dominions**: At the outbreak of World War II, Australia, Canada, New Zealand, and South Africa were independent nations. Their dominion status lay in the fact that they had the same monarch as Britain.

**Harrow School**: One of England's leading "public schools." These are, in effect, private prep schools. Founded in 1571, Harrow counts among its graduates many famous political and literary figures. In Churchill's day, Harrow ranked second perhaps only to Eton in prestige.

**Home Secretary**: When Churchill was Home Secretary from 1910 to 1911, he was the primary constitutional link between the king and the king's subjects living in Britain. In effect, the Home Secretary was in charge of law enforcement, prisons, pardons, labor, the care of foster children, censorship, and a further wide range of matters.

**India**: When Churchill entered Parliament in 1900, India was "the jewel in the crown of the British Empire." The king was emperor of India. India had its own army and civil service. The viceroy of India had more power than most European monarchs. World War I profoundly shook British power in India. By 1935, India was on its way to independence. Independence was achieved in 1947 but at the cost of division into India and Pakistan. Churchill was a staunch opponent of Indian independence.

**Ireland**: Until 1921, Ireland was part of Britain. As a result of negotiations in which Churchill played a major role, the Irish Free State was established as one of the British Dominions, like Canada. Only in 1949 did the Republic of Ireland come into existence as a completely independent nation, without any ties to Britain. This included only the southern four-fifths of Ireland; Northern Ireland remained part of the United Kingdom.

**Labour Party**: Founded in 1900, the British Labour Party was, at first, associated with the more radical elements of British liberalism. It moved ever more leftward, becoming, in effect, a socialist party, with a program of social insurance and nationalization of key industries.

**Lancaster, Duchy of**: This is the least prestigious post in the British Cabinet, responsible for appointing county magistrates. In disgrace as a result of the Dardanelles campaign, Churchill held the post briefly in 1915.

**Liberal Party**: The descendant of the 18th- and early 19th-century Whigs, the Liberals stood originally for the dominance of Parliament against the monarch. Individual liberty and free trade were the keystones of liberalism. William Gladstone dominated the Liberal Party from 1865 to 1895. The Liberals were for peace, as opposed to expansion of the Empire, and for the role of government in carrying out social welfare programs. The party's support of Home Rule, internal autonomy for Ireland, lost the support of its right wing. The rise of the Labour Party drew away its support on the left. After World War I, the Liberal Party played an increasingly minor role in British politics.

**Malakand**: District in northwest British India, now Pakistan; site of military campaign in 1897 in which Churchill saw action.

**Minister of Munitions**: In this post from 1917 to 1919, Churchill oversaw the production of munitions for the war effort. He brought order out of chaos, giving the British soldiers more than adequate supplies of weapons and shells. It also involved him in disputes with labor.

**Munich Conference**: From September 29–30, 1938, Chamberlain, Hitler, Mussolini, and the French Prime Minister Daladier met in Munich to resolve the crisis between Germany and Czechoslovakia over the Czech territory of the Sudentenland. To avoid war,

Chamberlain and Daladier completely capitulated to Hitler. Germany occupied the Sudentenland and, within six months, Hitler occupied the rest of Czechoslovakia.

**Omdurman**: Village in the Sudan; site of battle fought on September 2, 1898, between British forces under Kitchener and Sudanese forces. Omdurman was the capital of the religious and military leader known as the Mahdi (d. 1885). The victory at Omdurman removed the stain on British honor brought about by the Mahdi's capture of Khartoum and the death of the British general Charles Gordon in 1885.

**Parliament**: See Lecture Two.

**Sandhurst**: Royal Military College; founded in 1802, Sandhurst is the British equivalent of West Point.

**Secretary of War and Air**: In this post from 1919 to 1921, Churchill was in charge of Britain's military and air policy. This included the demobilization of millions of troops from the army. From this post, Churchill advocated military intervention against the Bolsheviks.

**Singapore**: In 1942, Singapore was a British colony and military base. Its capture by the Japanese ranks as the greatest defeat in British military history.

**Sudetenland**: Former name for northern portion of Czechoslovakia, which until the end of World War II, had a large German population. Hitler's determination to incorporate the Sudentenland into Germany precipitated the Munich Conference of 1938.

**wilderness**: "To be in the wilderness" is a British political term for a politician who is out of favor with his own party.

 ©2001 The Teaching Company.

# Biographical Notes

**Attlee, Clement** (1883–1967). British politician. Educated as an attorney, Attlee became active in social programs for boys and became a socialist in 1907. He served in World War I as a major. He was elected to Parliament in 1922 and, in 1931, became the leader of the Labour Party. In May 1940, the Labour Party refused to serve in a coalition government under Neville Chamberlain but did agree to serve under Churchill. This was critical to the appointment of Churchill as Prime Minister on May 10, 1940. Attlee served as Churchill's Deputy Prime Minister during the war. He was mainly charged with domestic matters. In personality and style, he and Churchill were radically different. Attlee was modest in his tastes. Churchill reportedly said of him, "Attlee is a modest man with much to be modest about." However, Attlee was extremely supportive of Churchill and made a significant contribution to the success of the war effort. He defeated Churchill in the election of 1945 and served as Prime Minister until 1951, when he was defeated by Churchill. Attlee paid Churchill the tribute of calling him "the greatest Englishman of our time."

**Baldwin, Stanley** (1867–1947). British politician. Baldwin was the son of a wealthy businessman. Educated at Harrow and Cambridge University, he had a lifelong love of the classics. For 20 years, he was absorbed by his father's steel business. But after entering Parliament in 1908, he rose with some rapidity in the Conservative Party. With a short interruption, Baldwin was Prime Minister from 1923–1929 and, again, from 1935–1937. Baldwin was concerned with winning public office rather than with what he could do in the position. His main concern was cultivating public opinion and balancing budgets. He was deceitful and hypocritical He misled the British about their military strength. Churchill served under him as Chancellor of the Exchequer from 1925–1929. However, Baldwin later dealt with Churchill in a most malicious fashion, using him to win votes, then denying him a place in the Cabinet. Like Lord Halifax and Neville Chamberlain, Stanley Baldwin represented the lack of principle and moral integrity that marked British politics between the World Wars.

**Chamberlain, Neville** (1869–1940). British politician. Chamberlain came from a political family. His father, Joseph Chamberlain (1836–1914), was one of the most influential figures of his day in the

Conservative Party. Neville Chamberlain's elder brother, Austen (1863–1937), was Foreign Secretary under Stanley Baldwin (1924–1929). Neville Chamberlain at first followed a business career, then served in local politics, being elected mayor of Birmingham in 1915. He entered Parliament in 1918. He served as Chancellor of the Exchequer from 1931–1937, where he focused on a balanced budget. He succeeded Baldwin as Prime Minister in 1937. His policy of appeasing Hitler brought Britain into World War II and to the brink of ruin. By the time of the German invasion of France in May 1940, Chamberlain had utterly lost the confidence of Parliament. "In the name of God, go," one long-time friend announced to him in Parliament. Chamberlain was devoid of moral courage and foresight. He felt deeply threatened by Churchill's brilliance and did everything to undermine Churchill's reputation. By contrast, Churchill treated Chamberlain with great magnanimity and permitted him to serve as Lord President of the Cabinet until poor health forced Chamberlain's retirement in October 1940.

**Churchill, Clementine Hozier** (1885–1977). Wife of Winston Churchill. Clementine Churchill came from an aristocratic background. She was the granddaughter of the tenth Earl of Airlie and the great-granddaughter of the second Baron Stanley of Alderly. Her father had a distinguished career in the military, then in business. However, her parents were separated, and Clementine was brought up in relatively reduced circumstances. She studied at the Sorbonne. She was regarded as one of the most beautiful and accomplished debutantes of her day. Her mother and Churchill's mothers were friends, and there were other ties between the families. Clementine and Churchill were married on September 12, 1908. Their son, Randolph, wrote, "their love remained constant and abiding." However, Clementine also found Winston wearing and frequently took vacations apart from him. The couple had five children: Randolph, Sarah, Diana, Marigold, and Mary. Marigold died at the age of two. Diana committed suicide at the age of 54. Like all the children, Randolph was devoted to his father and wrote the first two volumes of his biography. But he failed in his attempt at a political career and suffered from alcoholism. Clementine served as a firm anchor throughout the ups and downs of Churchill's political life. More than Churchill, she was a shrewd judge of people and circumstances, and he relied heavily on her advice.

  ©2001 The Teaching Company.

**Churchill, Lady Randolph-Spencer** (1854–1921). The mother of Winston Churchill. Jeanette (Jennie) was born in Brooklyn, New York, the daughter of Clara and Leonard Jerome. The ancestors of Leonard Jerome had fought in George Washington's army during the Revolutionary War. Leonard Jerome was a lawyer, who became highly successful as a New York stockbroker. His family spent much of its time in Europe. Jennie met Lord Randolph Churchill in London, and they were married in 1874. In addition to Winston, they had a second son, John (1880–1947). As was common among Victorian aristocrats, Jennie engaged in discrete promiscuity. Among her friends was the Prince of Wales, later King Edward VII. After Lord Randolph's death in 1895, she married a man 20 years her junior. She then married for a third time at the age of 64, again to a younger man. She was impecunious, and for a period, the young Churchill had to send her money. Churchill adored her, and her friendships and connections were of some use to him in advancing his career in its early stages.

**Edward VIII** (1894–1972). King of Britain from the death of George V on January 20, 1936, until his abdication on December 10, 1936. As Prince of Wales, Edward represented the flaming youth of the roaring 20s. He refused to marry and reveled in his role as social and fashion arbiter. On becoming king, he made clear his intention to marry the American divorcee Mrs. Wallis Simpson. Equally clear was the determination of the Prime Minister, Stanley Baldwin, to prevent such a marriage. The anti-Americanism of the British ruling class played a major role in this antipathy to Wallis Simpson. There was also a general feeling, held by his mother, the queen, that Edward was unsuited to the role of monarch. A constitutional crisis was averted when Edward abdicated. Churchill sought to defend Edward and encouraged him to fight for his position. Churchill saw this as a matter of principle, but it damaged his reputation and popularity severely. After his abdication, Edward married Wallis Simpson, and as the Duke and Duchess of Windsor, they lived in exile from Britain. Edward was suspected of pro-German sympathies. When the war broke out, he was appointed to the military mission in France, with the rank of major-general. After the fall of France, he made his way with his wife to Lisbon. There were rumors of a German plot to kidnap them. However, nothing came of this, and the Duke of Windsor served as governor of the Bahamas from 1940 until 1945. Churchill's consistent defense of Edward is one of many instances of his loyalty and magnanimity.

**Eisenhower, Dwight David** (1890–1969). American general and President of the United States. Eisenhower rose from modest circumstances to the pinnacle of success in both his careers, as a soldier and as a politician. He led his country to victory in its greatest war, and he served with success for two terms as president. Unlike Patton, Eisenhower was not a battlefield commander. His skills were those of a supreme manager, precisely what was needed to bring about the cooperation of the Allied forces and the concentration of power necessary to defeat Germany. He and Churchill had an effective and cordial working relationship during he war, one that survived severe differences of opinion. In particular, Churchill was outraged that Eisenhower did not advance as far as possible into Germany to limit the extent of Soviet domination. Eisenhower and Churchill maintained their cordial relationship while working together as President and Prime Minister, but Eisenhower opposed Churchill in critical matters. He was determined to end British colonial rule. His refusal to have a summit conference with Churchill and the Soviet leaders brought a disappointing end to Churchill's last effort as Prime Minister.

**Halifax, Lord** (1881–1959). British politician. An aristocrat, he was educated at Eton and Oxford and served in World War I. Halifax was a leading member of the Conservative Party under Stanley Baldwin and Neville Chamberlain. He was appointed Viceroy of India, a post of enormous prestige. He worked assiduously to overcome the conflicts between Hindus and Muslims. His skills and instincts were largely those of a diplomat. Halifax admired Hitler and his achievements in bringing law and order to Germany and in suppressing communism. He was the first member of the British Cabinet to pay a personal visit to Hitler and became personal friends with leading Nazis. Antony Eden resigned in 1938 over Chamberlain's policy of appeasement. Halifax then became Foreign Secretary, equivalent to our Secretary of State, and was a vigorous supporter of Chamberlain in his efforts to avoid war with Germany. Halifax was an anti-Semite and otherwise utterly lacking in political principles. He represented the bankruptcy of British foreign policy under Neville Chamberlain. He was the choice of King George and Chamberlain to succeed Chamberlain as Prime Minister in May 1940. Realizing the difficulty of the situation, Chamberlain refused and recommended Churchill. In 1940, Churchill got him out of the Cabinet by appointing him ambassador to the United States. In that position, Chamberlain performed well, negotiating the lend-lease agreement and taking part in the founding of the United Nations. Lord Halifax died old and full of honors.

**Hitler, Adolf** (1889–1945). German dictator (1933–1945). Hitler, like Stalin, was the antithesis of Churchill. Born in modest circumstances in the Austro-Hungarian Empire, he shared Churchill's lack of success as a student. He failed in his attempt at a career in art, and at the outbreak of World War I, he was a vagabond in Munich. He fed on the misery of the German people after their defeat in the First World War to rise to a position of absolute power. From the beginning, Churchill recognized the evil represented by Hitler: "This wicked man, the repository and embodiment of many forms of soul-destroying hatreds, this monstrous product of former wrongs and shame." Even before Hitler came to power, Churchill spoke out against the wrong of anti-Semitism in Germany. Hitler refused to meet Churchill in 1932, regarding him as lacking any influence in British politics. Later, Hitler would recognize Churchill as his most unrelenting and dangerous enemy. The Holocaust and the destruction of much of Europe, including Germany, are testimony to what happens when a nation and its leader loses the moral compass. Hitler's suicide on April 30, 1945, further testified to the innate cowardice of a tyrant.

**Kitchener, Horatio Herbert** (1850–1916). Lord Kitchener was one of the most formidable military figures of Britain in the late 19th and early 20th centuries. His victory at Omdurman established him as the preeminent soldier of his age in the eyes of the British public: Kitchener of Khartoum. His leadership led to victory in the Boer War, where he pursued a ruthless strategy. He served with equal distinction and success in India and Egypt. When World War I broke out, his enormous personal prestige led him to be appointed head of the War Office. The force of his personality and his reputation made him the dominant figure in the conduct of the war, until his death at sea en route to Russia. Kitchener and Churchill clashed early and often. As Churchill said, "it was a case of dislike before first sight." Churchill served under Kitchener at Omdurman and criticized him severely in his book *The River War*. Churchill considered Kitchener "a vulgar, common man." Kitchener and Churchill were frequently at odds over strategy in World War I. However, Churchill took great comfort in Kitchener's words to him at the time of the Dardanelles crisis: Because of Churchill, when war came "the fleet was ready."

**Lloyd George, David** (1863–1945). British statesman. Lloyd George was born of Welsh parents of modest means. He became a lawyer and rose rapidly in politics. As a Liberal in Parliament, he became the close associate of Winston Churchill in the years immediately before World War I. In December 1916, he became Prime Minister. Against advice, he brought Churchill back into the government in 1917 as Minister of Munitions. Lloyd George led Britain to victory in the Great War and played a major role in the Versailles Peace Conference. The problems of Britain in the aftermath of World War I proved too much for his leadership and for the Liberal Party. His reputation was also permanently damaged by allegations of financial misconduct. At the outbreak of World War II, his position was curious, and he seemed to be among those in favor of a negotiated peace with Hitler. His relationship with Churchill was complex. He supported Churchill at several critical points, but he also privately expressed the feeling that Churchill would never get to the top of British politics because he did not inspire trust. In his eulogy to Lloyd George, Churchill said, "When the English history of the first quarter of the 20th century is written, it will be found that the greater part of our fortunes in war and peace were shaped by this one man."

**Montgomery, Field Marshal Sir Bernard** (1887–1976). British general. Montgomery was Britain's most famous and most controversial general of World War II. Badly wounded in 1914, Montgomery was a staff officer during much of World War I. He developed a very methodical approach to command, one that focused one reducing his casualties to a minimum by concentrating maximum support for his troops and by the most careful planning. He neither smoked nor drank, and his arrogance and abrasive manner made him many enemies throughout his career. His leadership of the British forces at El Alamein in the fall of 1942 was a turning point in the war. However, his failure to pursue the Germans was criticized by Churchill, and his generalship in Sicily and Italy was also controversial. Nonetheless, Montgomery was Allied land commander of the Normandy invasion. His attempt to outflank the Germans in September 1944 led to the disastrous operation known as Market-Garden. This and Montgomery's difficulties in cooperating with the Americans nearly led to his dismissal, but his public

 ©2001 The Teaching Company.

reputation made this impossible. He led his armies to victory, and on May 4, 1945, the German forces in northwestern Germany, the Netherlands, and Denmark surrendered to him on the Luneburg Heath. For his achievements, he was ennobled as Viscount Montgomery of Alamein.

**Roosevelt, Franklin Delano Roosevelt** (1882–1945). President of the United States (1933–1945). Churchill first met Roosevelt at the close of World War I when Roosevelt was serving in the Department of the Navy. Churchill admired the leadership that Roosevelt brought to the United States during the Great Depression, and he admired the bold program of social reform called the New Deal. At the outbreak of war with Germany in 1939, Roosevelt asked Churchill, then First Lord of the Admiralty, to keep him informed. Churchill assiduously developed personal ties with Roosevelt into "a most intimate association." This personal relationship undoubtedly played a role in Roosevelt's willingness to give ever greater aid to Britain before the entry of the United States into the war. Personally, Churchill and Roosevelt had much in common in terms of background and personal tastes. In his eulogy to Roosevelt, Churchill spoke of his "admiration for him as a statesman, a man of affairs, and a war leader, his upright, inspiring character, and his generous heart." To Churchill, Roosevelt was "the greatest American friend" Britain had ever known.

**Stalin, Joseph** (1879–1953). Dictator of the Soviet Union. Born in Georgia as Iosif Vissarionovich Djugashvili, Stalin ranks with Hitler as the most brutal and bloody dictator of the 20th century. Unlike Hitler, Stalin was, as the world judges these matters, a success. He led his country to victory in its greatest war. Because of him, the Soviet Union won the peace, becoming master over an empire in Eastern Europe and imposing the communist system over a considerable portion of the globe, including China. He made the Soviet Union into an industrial and a nuclear power. He died in power and in bed. No two leaders could be more different, as individuals and as statesmen, than Churchill and Stalin. The Soviet dictator personified Churchill's definition of a tyrant (Lecture Eleven). Stalin wanted power for the sake of power. He had no moral compass. However, during World War II, Churchill believed it essential to work with Stalin, even though he was under no illusions about the dictator. Stalin was, in Churchill's view, "an unnatural man, who would bring grave troubles and bloody consequences." It was a tragedy for the Western democracies that Roosevelt did not accept Churchill's judgment and act on it to prevent Soviet expansion at the close of the war.

**Truman, Harry S.** (1884–1972). President of the United States (1945–1952). Truman came from a very different background than Churchill or Roosevelt. Raised in the most modest circumstances and regarded as a political hack, he rose to the challenge in some of the most trying times faced by any president. He first met Churchill at the Potsdam Conference in July 1945. He at first impressed Churchill as tougher with Stalin than Roosevelt had been. Later, however, Churchill would bemoan the weakness of policy by which Truman had failed to use the threat of the atomic bomb to deter Soviet expansion. Truman disavowed Churchill's Iron Curtain speech. Churchill's second term as Prime Minister brought the two together again. Truman regarded Churchill as belonging to another era, out of touch with reality, overly loquacious but still on occasion, capable of great insight.

 ©2001 The Teaching Company.

# Bibliography

**Essential Reading:**

Blake, Robert, and Louis, Wm. Roger. *Churchill*. Oxford: Clarendon Press, 1993. Essays by leading scholars. The best guide to the view of Churchill current among academic historians.

Cannadine, David, editor. *Blood, Toil, Tears, and Sweat: The Speeches of Winston Churchill*. Boston: Houghton Mifflin, 1989. An excellent selection of Churchill's most important speeches.

Charmley, John. *Churchill: The End of Glory*. New York: Harcourt Brace, 1993. A biography that is critical of Churchill and represents the revisionist viewpoint. Highly selective in its use of material.

Churchill, Randolph. *Winston S. Churchill*. Volumes I–II. Boston: Houghton Mifflin, 1966–1967. The first two volumes of the official biography were written and written well by Churchill's son, Randolph. They carry the story to the outbreak of World War I. The volumes are accompanied by five companion volumes of documents.

Churchill, Winston. *The Second World War*. Volumes I–VI. Boston: Houghton Mifflin, 1948–1954. Churchill's memoirs of the war years. The work is essential to anyone who wants to understand Churchill, but the citation of documents is so intense that the volumes make for hard and, at times, boring reading.

D'Este, Carlo. *Patton: A Genius for War*. New York: Harper, 1995. A superb biography of the best American fighting general of World War II.

Gilbert, Martin. *Churchill: A Life*. New York: Henry Holt, 1991. The best one-volume biography of Churchill.

———. *Churchill: A Photographic Portrait*. New York: Wings Books, 1993. An excellent introduction to Churchill through photographs and quotations from his writings and speeches.

———. *Churchill's Political Philosophy*. New York: Oxford University Press, 1981. A brilliant summary, much of it in Churchill's own words, of his political principles.

———. *The Second World War*. New York, Henry Holt, 1989. A convenient and detailed one-volume history.

———. *Winston S. Churchill*. Volumes III–VIII. Boston: Houghton Mifflin, 1971–1988. Gilbert completed the massive official biography begun by Churchill's son, carrying Churchill's life from

World War I until his death in 1965. Gilbert's style is dry, but his work represents the most detailed and best biography of Churchill.

Manchester, William. *The Last Lion: Winston Spencer Churchill: Alone, 1932–1940*. Boston: Little, Brown and Company, 1988. These two volumes by Manchester represent the best—but an incomplete—biography of Churchill. They rank among the most masterful biographies in the English language.

———. *The Last Lion: Winston Spencer Churchill: Visions of Glory, 1874–1932*. Boston: Little, Brown and Company, 1983.

*Oxford Companion to the Second World War*. Edited by I. C. B. Dear. Oxford: Oxford University Press, 1995. Essential reference work for anyone seriously interested in World War II. Insightful articles on Churchill, Roosevelt, and Stalin as war leaders.

Taylor, A. J. P., editor. *Churchill Revised. A Critical Assessment*. New York: Dial Press, 1969. Essays by leading historians, presenting a balanced view of Churchill's achievements.

**Supplementary Reading:**

Alldritt, Keith. *The Greatest of Friends: Franklin D. Roosevelt and Winston Churchill, 1941–45*. New York: St. Martin, 1995. A good treatment of the personal and political relationship between the two Allied leaders.

Ambrose, Stephen. *D-Day*. New York: Simon and Schuster, 1995. A critically acclaimed account of June 6, 1944, by America's preeminent military historian.

Ashley, M. *Churchill as Historian*. New York: Scribner, 1968. A well-regarded study of Churchill's historical writings.

Barrett, Buckely. *Churchill: A Concise Bibliography*. Westport, Connecticut, 2000. An extremely valuable resource and the best place to start a serious study of Churchill.

Berlin, Isaiah. *Mr. Churchill in 1940*. London: John Murray, 1964. A highly sympathetic portrait of Churchill's political courage and brilliance by one of Britain's leading intellectuals.

Bullock, Alan, *Hitler: A Study in Tyranny*. New York: Harper, 1964. Still the best biography of Hitler.

Carlton, David. *Churchill and the Soviet Union*. New York/Manchester: Manchester University Press, 2000. Essential to an understanding of Churchill, his view of and relationship with communism and the Soviet Union.

Charmley, John. *Churchill's Grand Alliance: The Anglo-American Special Relationship, 1940–1957*. New York: Harcourt Brace, 1995. An important study of British-American relations during World War II and the Cold War. Critical both of Churchill and the United States.

Churchill, Winston. *Lord Randolph Churchill*. New York: MacMillan, 1906. Rightly called "one of the most interesting political biographies in the English language," this is an important source for understanding Churchill's own view of politics, as well as his image of his father.

―――. *Marlborough, His Life and Times*. New York: Charles Scribner's Sons, 1933–1938. Brilliantly written, this is one of the best biographies in the English language. The life of Marlborough profoundly influenced Churchill and his ideas of leadership.

―――. *Painting as a Pastime*. London: Odhams Press, 1948. Churchill's sensitive and insightful comments on the hobby he made into a vocation.

―――. *A Roving Commission: My Early Life*. New York: Charles Scribner's Sons, 1930. Churchill's delightful account of his life until his entry into Parliament.

―――. *The World Crisis*. Volumes I–V. New York: Charles Scribner's Sons, 1923–1931. Churchill's memoirs of the World War I era. It is more well written and more enjoyable reading than his history of World War II.

Clayton, Tim, and Craig, Phil. *Finest Hour: The Battle of Britain*. New York: Simon and Schuster, 1999. A highly recommended and detailed account of one of the supreme episodes in Churchill's career.

Foster, R. F. *Lord Randolph Churchill: A Political Life*. Oxford: Clarendon Press, 1981. The best scholarly study of Churchill's father.

Halle, Kay. *Irrepressible Churchill: Stories, Sayings and Impressions of Winston Churchill*. New York: Facts on File, 1985. One of several collections illustrating the human side of Churchill.

Hamilton, Nigel. *Monty*. Volumes I–III. New York: McGraw-Hill, 1981–1987. A monumental biography of this most controversial and important British general of World War II.

James, Robert Rhodes. *Churchill: A Study in Failure*. New York: World Publishing Company, 1970. A seminal example of the revisionist view of Churchill, highly influential on the biography by John Charmley.

Jones, J. R. *Marlborough*. Cambridge: Cambridge University Press, 1993. A recent scholarly survey of Marlborough and his career.

Lamb, Richard. *Churchill as War Leader: Right or Wrong*. London: Bloomsbury, 1993. A recent discussion of positive and negative perspectives of Churchill's achievement in wartime.

Lewin, Ronald. *Churchill as Warlord*. New York: Stein and Day, 1973. A valuable study of Churchill's leadership in wartime.

Lukacs, John. *Five Days in London: May 1940*. New Haven: Yale University, 1997. A fascinating account of a critical moment in history and Churchill's role in it.

Muller, James. *Churchill's Iron Curtain Speech Fifty Years Later*. Columbia, Missouri: University of Missouri Press, 1999. A collection of scholarly essays, placing the speech in its historical context and judging its impact.

Overy, R. J. *The Battle of Britain: The Myth and the Reality*. New York: Norton, 2001. A good survey and reappraisal of the events and significance of what is generally regarded as a turning point in World War II.

Patton, George S. *War as I Knew It*. New York: Bantam, 1980. A watered-down version of Patton's diaries, published after his death but still giving intriguing insights into the man and his character.

Rasor, Eugene L. *Winston Churchill 1874–1965: A Comprehensive Historiographical and Annotated Bibliography*. Westport, Connecticut: Greenwood Press, 2000. A major research tool of enormous value for anyone with a serious interest in Churchill.

Sandys, Celia. *Churchill: Wanted Dead or Alive*. New York: Carroll and Graf, 2000. A retelling of Churchill's escapades during the Boer War by one of his descendants.

Soames, Mary. *Winston and Clementine: The Personal Letters of the Churchills*. Boston: Houghton Mifflin, 1999. A fascinating portrait of Churchill as a husband and a family man.

———. *Winston Churchill: His Life as a Painter*. Boston: Houghton Mifflin, 1990. An excellent discussion of Churchill's artistic work in the context of his life.

Stafford, David. *Roosevelt and Churchill: Men of Secrets*. Woodstock, New York: Overlook Press, 2000. A reconsideration of the character of Churchill and Roosevelt and their impact on World War II.

Young, John W. *Winston Churchill's Last Campaign: Britain and the Cold War*. Oxford: Clarendon Press, 1996. The best treatment of Churchill and his struggle against communism and Soviet expansion.

Sept 28   2 to 3:30
AARP Fraud Basic

Friday 8/30 — 12 noon
online.